START YOUR STARTUP RIGHT

Start Your Startup Right

BUSINESS POSTS FROM A JOURNEYMAN ENTREPRENEUR

Gregory M. Coticchia

ISBN-13: 9780692950647
ISBN-10: 0692950648
Library of Congress Control Number: 2017914760
Gregory M. Coticchia, McMurray, PA

Greg Coticchia is a seasoned marketing executive and serial entrepreneur who has been there and done that. He offers, sound, proven, and practical advice on the full spectrum of marketing challenges. This book offers valuable guidance for executives in organizations of any size—from start-up to Fortune 500.

~ Peter Horst, Previous SVP, Brand Marketing,
Capital One and Chief Marketing Officer,
The Hershey Company

If you don't read Greg's compendium of thoughtful essays and don't take his sage advice, your impending failure is on you. If, conversely, you do both of the above and things still go awry, at least you'll have someone else to blame. :)

~ Chris Rasmussen, Founder and CEO,
Deadeye Marketing

Through a series of blog posts, personal anecdotes and years of experience, Greg has accomplished what many have tried and failed to do. Greg has captured the essence of a marketer's job. You don't have to be an entrepreneur to gain value. Sales and marketing newbies to worn out execs can benefit from Greg's insights, guidance and prescriptions.

~ Hinda Chalew, Director, Analyst Relations,
Netscout

Product managers and intrapreneurs will love Greg Coticchia's new book, *Start Your Startup Right: Business Posts from A Journeyman Entrepreneur."* As Greg says it's not enough to study or think about a new idea you have to "get bloodied." In 30 years Greg has amassed a wealth of experience in all things sales, marketing and innovation and now he shares it with you.

~ Mark Adkins, President, Smart Hammer Innovation
and Adjunct Professor, Pitt Center for
Medical Innovation

Building a great business, product or service is a journey, not a destination, and Greg has assembled a useful compilation of thought-provoking insights and lessons learned through decades of experience building multiple businesses.

~ John Becker, Former Chief Executive Officer,
Sourcefire

TABLE OF CONTENTS

DEDICATION

To *real* entrepreneurs and product managers: Long may you
fight the good fight.

Author's Bio

Greg Coticchia, MBA, PC, is an award-winning, technology executive with more than 30 years' experience in high-tech products and services. He currently serves the University of Pittsburgh as its Director of the Startup Accelerator, "The Blast Furnace," as Director of the University of Pittsburgh's Innovation Institute, and as an Executive in Residence (EIR) for software and information technology.

Greg has led or been a major contributor to two of the largest and most successful software companies in the world, LEGENT (now CA) and AXENT (now Symantec). He has been involved in 14 start-ups, has founded 4, has held executive positions for better than two-thirds of his career, and has participated in various size organizations, from startup to more than $1 billion in revenue.

Throughout his career, Greg has participated in raising more than $73 million in venture capital, and has actively participated in more than 17 mergers and acquisitions at the corporate and product levels. He has served as CEO 4 times, as President and COO, and has been involved or responsible for the launch of more than 100 products and solutions.

A graduate of the University of Pittsburgh in Industrial Engineering, Greg received his MBA also at the University of Pittsburgh. He currently teaches several courses including B2B Marketing at the University of Pittsburgh Katz School of Business. He holds certificates in Entrepreneurial Management from Carnegie Mellon University and Professional Coaching from Duquesne University.

Greg was named as a finalist 3 times for the Ernst and Young Entrepreneur of the Year Award and for the Tech 50 CEO of the Year. He was also named a 2006 Distinguished Graduate of the University of Pittsburgh (Katz).

ACKNOWLEDGEMENTS

I 've been lucky in many ways. And if anyone has had any success in any area of life and has said that he or she hasn't been lucky, that's just plain lying. Yes, you can make your own luck through working hard, so you are in the right place at the right time. But there's no doubt that plain, old-fashioned luck, the kind with no explanation, does play a role.

One of the many ways I've been lucky is relating to all the wonderful people who have helped me along the way in my career, who have given me a chance to help them, and to learn myself, and who have contributed to the thoughts and entries in this book.

This book is a compilation of my thoughts, opinions, experiences and observations. I chose, over a period of several years, to share them on a series of LinkedIn posts. They turned out to be much more popular reads than I anticipated. So here they are, all in one place, plus some additional ones not published before.

I can't possibly thank everyone who has impacted my thoughts in marketing, product management, business development, startups, entrepreneurship, leadership, and more. We each have a journey with many people who impact us along the way. These relationships have led to my forming these thoughts and experiences.

Here are a few I want to thank: Ed Lasure (a great first manager), Bruce DaCosta (for giving me a chance), Ravi Ghai (a true marketing genius and great mentor), C.W. Park (a great prof), Neal Pollon (I learned so much from you.), Greg Strouse (for showing me the ropes) John Parillo (a great sales leader and friend), Marc Shinbrood (a friend and mentor), Brett Jackson (You pushed me hard to be better than I thought I could be.), John Becker (a great friend and boss), Alan Himler (a true friend and someone I admire, respect and have learned much from), Bob Delach (for keeping me on track so many times), Dani Garcia and Gabby Isturiz (Thanks for the opportunity to apply what I knew and to see it work).

I also want to thank two important former teams of mine: My team at Duquesne Systems/LEGENT and my team at AXENT. I really think there were no better teams in marketing and product management. You excelled as individuals and teams, and your results stood the test of time. It's very satisfying to see so many of you succeed in your careers. You taught me a lot, and I hope I served you well.

I also want to thank my students at the University of Pittsburgh. I've been so fortunate to teach at many schools: Carnegie Mellon University, Duquesne University and Phoenix University. But most important, I've taught at my alma mater, the University of Pittsburgh, at the graduate and undergraduate levels. My students have all taught me and challenged me as much as I have hopefully done the same for them.

I want to thank Hank Walshak and Henry Wilde for helping me edit this book and for getting it done with me. And I thank Barbara Thomas for inspiring me to finally do it.

And of course, I want to thank my wife, Kelly. You've lived it. All of it. Thank you.

FORWARD

I first met Greg Coticchia in an interview late in 1999. He was Senior Vice President of Marketing, and I was interviewing for the Lead Generation Manager position on his team. I knew immediately from that meeting, I wanted to grow up and be just like him. I wanted him to be my mentor, learning whatever he was willing to teach and share with me.

As I entered his office, Greg came out from behind his desk, shook my hand with force, pulling me in towards him a bit, smiling ear to ear and looking straight at me. He leaned in, encroaching on my personal space, radiating a positive energy and walking with me toward a table in his office where two chairs were located. He motioned me to sit down and started the interview immediately by saying, "Tell me all about yourself," before my butt even hit the chair seat.

We sat side by side at a round table in his office as I answered his questions directly, sharing any story I could with metrics of success throughout my career. Greg's excitement about lead-generation marketing and database management was contagious. We talked about what marketing should be, what strategies should be employed, and what best-in-class technology should be leveraged. We were in sync that first meeting and have been ever since.

Yes, I got the job, but I received so much more. I got a mentor, a treasured resource, a valued partner, and a life-time friend. Throughout my career, the knowledge, wisdom and insights he shared have improved my career and work experiences. Greg made me feel as if he saw more capabilities in me than I did in myself. He would challenge me and give me problems to solve in any way possible. He expected me to push the envelope, get out of my comfort zones and not fear failure. It was the best way to learn.

I followed Greg from the first job to his next company where he served as COO. He brought me in to help structure the marketing department and build a new team to grow the small, security company. The firm was struggling with few leads and processing any that did come in within days rather than seconds. We brought in marketing processes and tools.

Around this time, one of my favorite emails came from Greg. Within this email, Greg wrote, "We are making progress. We have gone from "we have no leads" to "all our leads are crap." This is forward momentum. We are headed in the right direction." He continued on within the email about sales and marketing needing agreement on profiling and defining lead quality and creating sales stages.

Greg's knowledge of all areas of business is more than impressive. His knowledge and skills to take an idea, support it, pitch it, develop and expand it are rare to find in one person. His ability to discern and judge which aspects of business are right, lasting and applicable make Greg a source of wisdom and insight. His deep experience demonstrates knowing the meaning or reason of why something works versus why it misses the mark.

I've continued to admire Greg's ability to knock down road blocks in business, to seek positive solutions, to encourage people to try and to rejuvenate teams with his optimistic energy.

The stories Greg shares within these pages encapsulate the knowledge, wisdom, and insights I wanted after that first interview with him. It's all the information I wanted to tap into so many years ago. Consider yourself privileged to have direct and immediate access to Greg's wealth of business experience.

Barbara Thomas, CDM, CeM
Creative Tactics, LLC

INTRODUCTION

I always wanted to write a book to share my thoughts on the subjects I care about most–startups, entrepreneurship, Business-to-Business (B2B) marketing, and the modern workplace.

I didn't originally plan on writing a book by posting on LinkedIn. But in this era of *agile, lean* and especially *iteration* as methods to build something, it made sense for me to use my LinkedIn posts to stitch together the book I'd always wanted to write.

So, what's the essence of this book? Think of it as a straightforward and contemporary Master's course that takes you, the reader, from business idea to commercialization for a product, a service, or a company. Once you complete your reading, you don't get a diploma, but you will receive insights and practical advice I've gained from winning and losing over the years on the real "battlefields" of entrepreneurship.

Speaking of entrepreneurship, I've participated in 14 small businesses and startups, and I've advised hundreds of startup entrepreneurs as a consultant, advisor or board member. The advice you'll read about here is practical, but applying it can be challenging. The more I interact with early-stage businesses, the more I see the same pattern of changes they face, and the similar decisions they have to make about many of the issues I address here.

I grew up at a time when the word, "entrepreneur," meant you were out of work. Being an entrepreneur wasn't respected and celebrated as a profession the way it is today. Now, we enjoy entire ecosystems dedicated to helping entrepreneurs build their businesses.

If they knew what they were really getting into, many entrepreneurs wouldn't do it. One of my close friends, Larry Shoup, an entrepreneur himself, often says that being an entrepreneur is like putting your head in a vice and turning it slowly every day.

It's painful to create something new. And an entrepreneur who launches a startup lives under multilayered responsibilities: To customers in a market. To sources of funding. To employees. To oneself. To one's life partner, and perhaps, children. Plus, we face multiple, stakeholder needs, and these needs aren't always aligned.

And we need help that can be delivered in as many ways as possible. One such way is this book. Think of it as a go-to guide. Without such a guide for starting and keeping a startup going, being an entrepreneur is like being an actor in a play who acts without learning beforehand the characters and lines of a play, but must learn the lines as he or she goes along in the play.

Through writing the book as individual posts over time, I've been able to focus on individual subjects consistently for the startup entrepreneur to know about without being distracted by some large overarching subject matter or framework. I believe this makes each read more meaningful, and the book, more useful. Readers needn't go from the first page until the end to get value. They can read about whichever topic interests them the most at different times.

The process of posting on LinkedIn makes me grateful for those who wrote me or called me about the original posts, or who commented on the posts, and gave me and readers even further insight that could be incorporated into this book version.

You'll find this book filled with practical examples of what a startup entrepreneur should and should not do during startup time. This includes the all-time classic of having a "product that sells itself" –no product sells itself– in the post, "Your Business Strategy: By Design or Default?" … or underestimating your competition, or thinking you don't have any, in the piece, "Never Underestimate Your Competition" … or understanding the role emotions play in all buying decisions–even in a B2B setting–in the post, "Of Washing Machines and Dryers: Why the Customer Isn't Always King."

Not every article here is directly about starting a business, but I promise these articles will be useful to you in the various stages of your entrepreneurial career. For example, the article, "Should Pitch Competitions Die?" is one of my favorites. On the surface, this article discusses pitch contests and how popular they've become.

You may be asked to mentor a team, or serve as a judge at one of these events. Hopefully, this post will give you insight on how to make them better for participates and most important, how they can produce better results, just like a good startup.

Finally, let me say something about the title of this book, *Start Your Startup Right: Posts from a Journeyman Entrepreneur.*" What's a journeyman? Well, first of all, the term, "journeyman" doesn't have to be a man, but the term, "journeyperson," has yet to be coined or used, and I'm not a "journeywoman."

More directly, Wikipedia–the source of all truth, because we know crowd sourced intelligence is always accurate ☺– states that "In American English, a journeyman or journeywoman is an athlete who's technically competent but unable to excel." The term is used elsewhere.

In British and Australian contexts, "journeyman" is used to refer to a professional athlete who plays for a large number of different clubs during his career. Such a player is typically signed to year-by-year contracts, and may be signed by a team to fill in for an injured starter. As a rule, the term is used pejoratively. There have been many great journeyman athletes in every sport, and many who played on teams or led teams that won championships.

In many ways, I feel my career as an entrepreneur has been as a journeyman. I don't, however, consider this a pejorative term at all, or that I am unable to excel and am only technically competent. These considerations aside, I have, as my mother would say, been professionally promiscuous.

I've been with many companies, launched hundreds of products and services, and advised many startup entrepreneurs. I like to say, "I've seen a lot of movies." As a result, I feel I can add more value than the one-and-done entrepreneur, or even the one who has only experienced a handful of startups. My hope with this book is that you'll gain from my multiple experiences as reflected in the insights and advice I offer.

Thank you for choosing to spend your time with these thoughts and opinions of mine. I hope you find them helpful and useful. And let me know what you think. I can be reached at gregcott@gmail.com or on twitter @GregCott.

Regards,
Greg Coticchia

SECTION 1: HOW TO LAUNCH YOUR BUSINESS

CHOOSE WISELY. JUST BECAUSE YOU CAN PICK UP A PENCIL DOESN'T MEAN YOU CAN WRITE

Gee, it looks so easy, that marketing stuff. It really can't be that hard, can it? Looks mostly administrative. Organize this, plan that, order this, etc. We can get an administrative person, a secretary, to do most of it. Save a lot of money that way.

And of course, there's the creative stuff. Well, that's overrated, and I like to think of myself as a creative person. I mean it's like interior decorating, right? I've done that for my house, and other people love the way I've done my house. I'm good at picking colors. I have a knack for it I guess. And heck, I have a college degree, so I can do the heavy lifting. And we can do the marketing that way.

I hear echoes like this all the time from start-up entrepreneurs and early-stage company leaders. I even hear it in some larger companies where marketing isn't valued or established. Some don't even know the difference between marketing and sales.

A close friend of mine said that these folks tend to think of marketing as "color picking and taste fairying." She reminds me that just because you can pick up a pencil doesn't mean you can write. How true.

Let's start with something you need to understand and accept. Marketing– specifically marketing communications–is a profession. It's not a do-it-yourself thing, because you're smart, educated, and you think it looks easy.

There's a right way to do it. It takes an education plus skills that go beyond liking this or not liking that. And there's a right way to get results. And yes, these results can be measured. There's a science to it.

And the creative part has a science and a rationale. Marketing communications doesn't come to you by praying at the altar of the intellect.

Consider this recent example. A small, startup company gets some nice press coverage from a world-renowned blogger in its space. That's fantastic! It gets picked up on several, major news outlets like CNBC Business. That's even better. Kudos to the start up.

So, what could be done with this kind of coverage?

Well first, let's step back. First off, you can't plan everything, take advantage of, or leverage every opportunity, especially when it comes to external-events leverage.

Marketing should not be a one-time event. It's not a hit-and-run exercise. You may feel like you made a hit, and that's OK. Nonetheless, you need to prepare and to plan not only for events over which you have an internal locus of control, but also for those that come to you, and also when an external event, like getting press coverage, drives the opportunity.

Let's start with this idea: If you can use multiple marketing vehicles to emphasize your message, you have a better chance to be heard in the market by prospects and customers. And if they hear about your company with the same message in multiple media, that's effective.

The concept of integrated marketing communications has been around for better than 25 years. Yet, despite this, some startup companies still don't practice it.

(Integrated marketing communications is the application of consistent brand messaging across traditional and non-traditional marketing channels and using a variety of promotional methods that reinforce each other.)

The hard truth is that most people don't have the time or attention to devote to your business. And frankly they don't care about you or your business. They care about themselves. They believe in WIIFM–What's in It for Me. And the chances of your breaking through the noise of the market so they can hear about you is slim. And if they do hear about you and want to learn more, your message needs to be focused and consistent. How do we know all this is true?

The next time you get mail delivered to your home, stop and think about how much time you spend with each piece of mail you open or look at. Most people spend 2 to 3 seconds per piece, with most going in the garbage.

Now think about the cost to the company that produced that mail. Do you remember any of the mail you received a day later? Response and open rates for physical direct mail still hover at around 2 percent

Now, think about your routine with email. How much time do you spend looking through it? It's estimated that people spend 1 to 2 seconds per email, looking at the subject line. Open rates on email can range from a low of 8 percent to a high of 30 percent, depending on the marketing segment. Click-through rates hover around 7 percent. Do you remember any of these a day later?

And if your messages about your product or company do break through the clutter and you are read or heard, the last thing you need is to have your prospects get confused later on. You don't want them to read an email from you with a message that you fix problem A, and when they need a problem A fixer, they remember to go to your web site and see a lot of we-solve-problem-Z messages. All your other messaging and positioning needs to mutually leverage and to mutually reinforce through your media vehicles continually and consistently.

OK, let's say you can perform integrated marketing communications. Let's also say that something special–an external event-comes your way, like predicting who's being vetted for the Vice President selection in the U.S. presidential election a year ahead of time. That's cool if you're selling big-data analytics software. This shows the power of your offering.

So, what do you do? Do you simply give that news away to a powerful blogger and then post something similar on your blog on your web site? Absolutely not. You can, and should, do much more if you want to leverage it and maximize its value.

You need to use everything you have to match your message to your product or service offering. You need to use tools and vehicles of inbound marketing (Facebook, Twitter, LinkedIn) ads (Google Adwords, LinkedIn, etc.), email, webinars, your website, whitepapers, infographics, and the like. And yes, you even use events like trade shows.

Here's what you want to have happen: The target customer for your offering reads the article in a print medium or online, sees your mention and the reference to your product, refers to your company website which they go to and see that more can be read on your blog.

Later that day, your company sends the same target customer an email, with a call to action for the whitepaper you wrote on the subject and related information. Better yet, you direct your customer to a link on which your customer can register to watch a webinar about the same subject. Maybe you're exhibiting at an upcoming trade show, and you send an invite to visit you there, when your customer is looking for big-data-analytics software.

In this example, everything reinforces and leverages the content-marketing machine you have created. Even if you don't have an external event triggering the actions I have suggested in the example above, you still need to think through the execution of your marketing programs the same way.

Yes, this is administrative, but it's also strategic. And in today's quantitative, analytical marketing, you need to have a metric to gauge the success of every marketing vehicle and make every marketing action measurable.

You need to make sure you're not wasting money. The days of "half the money I spend on advertising is wasted; the trouble is I don't know which half" (John Wanamaker) are over! We know what's wasted in the digital-marketing age. Besides that, the content we build and spend money creating needs to be used wisely and measured for effectiveness.

When it comes to marketing, test everything. Your liking has nothing to do with it. Marketing is neither an administrative task, nor is it for amateurs.

STARTING A STARTUP: THE SCIENCE OF CREATING A NEW BUSINESS

I remember vividly my first startup, American Robot Corporation. I joined the company after a number of years in B2B sales, called *industrial sales* in those days. American Robot was a startup focused on the growing trend of factory automation so that United States companies could compete more effectively with Japan.

Back then, one of the ways for companies to compete was with robotic technology. It was exciting going to work in the morning and going to the back of our building, watching robots paint, seal, water-jet cut, pick and place, and other manufacturing activities.

Actually, I worked for a startup within the startup, American Industrial Vision Corporation, or AIVC. We were funded separately from our parent company, American Robot Corporation, affectionately called ARC. BMW Ventures had invested $5 million in us to build several different types of industrial, vision systems, including stand-alone and robotic systems.

This was heady stuff in 1986. In retrospect, it was like being back when dinosaurs roamed the earth. For manufacturers, operating systems, user interfaces, hardware components and much more lacked any real standardization or definition. This made doing real time vision analysis for inspection and quality control incredibly challenging.

I remember that the only camera technology we could use at the time implemented a 3 x 4-pixel technology. Compared with today's standardized technology, this was primitive. It was the same technology used in TV's and was analog based. The data had to be normalized (2 x 2), digitized, and then analyzed for quality defects in real time. Needless to say, this was challenging.

I went on to do a lot more startups, contributing in some manner to 14 in all to date. That's a lot of movies to see. And when you think about each one of them, they were all different, like children or snowflakes. Some were successful, some were failures. But they were all reaching to make a dent in the universe.

In my role now at a major research university, I help to create new startups. I find it incredibly rewarding and a lot of work. Like many things in life, it seems like it should be so simple from the outside, but moving research of student ideas to commercialization requires a lot of heavy lifting, so to speak.

What I've found most interesting about creating startups is the process as evidenced by venture capital in startups and the startup process itself.

By the way, as I write this, the United State is experiencing continuing love for all things entrepreneurial. One measure of all this is the amount of venture capital investment in startups. Venture In the first quarter of 2017, venture-capital backed companies saw $13.9 billion in total financing across 1,104 deals. This showed an uptick from the fourth quarter of 2016 to the tune of 15 percent in venture-capital investments and 2 percent in deals. This, according to the Money Tree™ Report by PricewaterhouseCoopers LLP (PwC).

We love entrepreneurs almost as much as we love our sports figures. The rags to riches and the overcoming-adversity stories of entrepreneurship, whether about Steve Jobs, or Andrew Carnegie, mesmerize us. And tales of successful entrepreneurs are told in books and movies, and are quoted liberally on the internet and through social media.

What has amazed me the most is how we're doing startups. We're getting better at it.

To me, it's much like the early days of the industrial revolution, when Frederick Taylor started the Scientific Management movement. He and his associates were the first people to study the work process scientifically. They studied how work was performed and they looked at how this affected worker productivity.

Taylor's philosophy focused on the belief that making people work as hard as they could was not as efficient as optimizing the way work was done. In 1909, Taylor published *The Principles of Scientific Management*. In this book, he proposed that productivity would increase by optimizing and simplifying jobs. He also advanced the idea that workers and managers needed to cooperate with one another. This was different in large measure from the way work was typically done in businesses beforehand.

In today's world of startups, something similar has emerged. We are scientifically building startups. If you haven't been following what's happening in the world of creating new businesses, the bottom line from my perspective involves these elements:

1.) **Testing:** We're now testing our hypotheses about our businesses, our value propositions, and our customers earlier in the process. This is probably the most significant change I see and read about on a consistent basis.

If you've not bought a copy of Alexander Osterwalder and Yves Pigneur's *Business Model Generation*, run, don't walk to Amazon and click to buy a copy. Despite my affection for reading only on Kindle, this book is better read in hard copy. The model is simple and brilliant. Essentially, it replaces a business plan and is also a living document that allows any entrepreneurial team to reduce risks, uncertainties and unknowns when it's put into action.

Last year, Osterwalder and his team went a step further and focused on Value Proposition Design. This terrific tool gets to the essence of any startup, small business, or new business idea: *"What's the value of what you're selling, or intend to sell, and who is the buyer or customer?"*

Value Proposition Design creates a testing process that eliminates the guesswork by asking the right questions. In business, bad news early is good news. Taken together, Osterwald's book, Business *Model Generation*, and Value Proposition Design allow the early-stage business to test its assumptions in a framework. They're brilliant.

2.) **Iterating**: We're iterating, and LEAN is in. I remember Glen Chatfield, cofounder of Duquesne Systems, my second startup, handing me a book in 1991 called *The Machine That Changed the World*. It was all about Toyota's LEAN production system. When *The Machine That Changed the World* was first published in 1990, Toyota was half the size of General Motors. Today, Toyota is passing General Motors as the world's largest auto maker and is the most consistently successful global enterprise of the past fifty years.

This management classic was the first book to reveal Toyota's LEAN production system that's the basis for its enduring success. LEAN is everywhere now. It's hot. The most popular work in startup land is Eric Ries's *The Lean Startup*. This book is an adaptation of LEAN for startups, and its approach is being adopted across the globe, changing the way companies are built and new products are launched.

By the way, Eric Ries defines a startup as an "organization dedicated to creating something new under conditions of extreme uncertainty." I love this definition, because it points to the issues of why we need to test and iterate to reduce risk and to get better outcomes.

3.) **Money:** We're spending less and getting more. Although we're raising more money overall for startups, as discussed earlier, we're spending less to achieve results, good or bad. In fact, we're doing more with less. While traditional seed round funding today ranges from $750,000 to $2 million from angel investors and seed funds, a typical Series A round falls within the range of $2 million to $10 million.

These numbers are significantly lower than they were more than 10 years ago. My startup at that time had raised $23 million in seed and Series A funding. That's an enormous difference and points to how we raise money, how much we need, and how we use it.

4.) **Process:** Processes, models and canvases exist to build startups. Going hand in hand with the first point about testing, we now have models to visualize how a startup business works or doesn't work. These models, often shown as a canvas, are tremendous tools. They are to startups what SWOT Analysis, Porter's Five Forces, or the Boston Consulting Group Growth Share Matrix are to strategy analysis and creation. I'm sure more will come.

One of my favorites is Bill Aulet's "Disciplined Entrepreneurship." This is a 24-step program for the process of building a startup. It's nicely done and walks a startup team from beginning to launch.

When I worked at companies like American Robot, we didn't have these tools, processes, or canvases. We did raise a lot of money and probably wasted a lot. These new ways of efficiently testing what we're doing and testing our assumptions and hypotheses are of tremendous value, not only for startups but also for new products created in existing businesses.

As an industrial engineer by training, I love that we are now applying "Taylor" to startups, and modern methods of scientific management to the ways we bring new businesses to life. As a veteran in startups, I'm well aware that risk looms at every corner. I applaud these modern-day business changes, and I welcome new ones.

Embrace it. We're getting better.

Strategy: The Four Questions

> *"If you don't know where you are going,*
> *any road will get you there."*
> ~ Lewis Carroll

Strategy. The word conjures distinct feelings. Some of us who are more operationally or action oriented think of hours in an offsite meeting spent eating stale doughnuts and over-warmed coffee, discussing four-quadrant charts with post-it notes on them, an overpaid facilitator, and long days better spent someplace, or someway, else.

"What an incredible waste of time," many of us think. "Nothing ever comes out of these meetings."

And yet, some of us look forward to these meetings, so we can finally get away from the day-to-day action of our business to reflect on what we believe we really need to do to get on the same page with our team. Oh, and of course, partake in the doughnuts and coffee.

Unfortunately, whether you enjoy or hate strategy meetings or somewhere in between, strategy itself is thought of as a squishy subject. For many of us, it's poorly defined. Or even something that we can delegate or even outsource.

So, let's step back and understand specifically what strategy is, so we can better use it. Because, whether we believe it or not, we have a strategy. It may be working or not. It may be explicit or implied. But we have one. So better to bring it out on the table and to discuss it.

I've heard lots of definitions of what strategy is. Several years back, I sat in a meeting where a wonderful speaker–an ex-CEO–discussed strategy in the context of a start-up. He provided what he called the four, basic questions of strategy. This was probably the best definition of strategy I had ever heard.

Here they are:

1. How attractive is the market?
2. Where will we compete?
3. How will we compete?
4. What is the financial impact?

I loved, and still love, these questions. They distill strategy into its basic parts.

In answer to the first question, attractiveness is measured by "is it large enough?" Large is measured by aspects like <u>market size</u>, <u>growth and profitability.</u>

The speaker I was watching looked for markets at least $2 billion in size. Why? Because large markets can absorb a lot of mistakes. Inevitably, large markets forgive us as we make mistakes and still allow us to win our share of the market.

That's important. If a market is too small, it can't absorb the risk or pay out the reward we expect as participants in the market. Remember, there's only one thing worse than no customers. That's one customer. So, think big!

The answer to the second question is choosing *where* to compete. The speaker suggested mapping the marketplace and making sure to understand the positioning of your products in the marketplace you've chosen. Good idea.

The answer to where will we compete comes down to segmentation. You can't be everything to everyone. You have to know who your customer is, and have real clarity around that.

To help, I suggest using the basic positioning statement outline contained in *Crossing the Chasm* by <u>Geoffrey Moore. If</u> you don't have a copy of this outline, here it is:

- For (target customers)
- Who must (solve a specific problem)
- Our product is a new (new product category)
- That provides (key breakthrough benefit vs. current way of doing things, which solves a dilemma.)
- Unlike (competitor in new category)
- We have (whole product most relevant for you)

Here's a good exercise: Have your team in charge of strategy complete the positioning statement separately. Then, have them bring their positioning statements to a meeting and read them out loud.

My experience tells me that you will be shocked by the differences and by the similarities. And then, get to work to create one you can all agree to and work with moving forward.

The third question about how we will compete is an attempt to answer, "Why us?" I like to frame the answer in response to two, more direct questions: Why do we deserve to be in business? What would customers do if we weren't in business?

These questions may sound harsh, but they go to the essence of understanding how we will compete in the market. In thinking through how we will compete, we need to address the classic 4P's of marketing-Product, Place, Promotion and Price, separately as well as together.

Are we competing on price? Do we have something unique in the market? Is that uniqueness valued by prospects? In what way? By saving time? Saving money? Adding to their unique capabilities?

So, think through what is your unfair advantage. And get clarity around it. And don't list 10 or 20 items. Think of one or two that give you your competitive advantage.

Last is the financial-impact question: What is the expected revenue and associated profit from the potential investment. If we know the market size and opportunity, and we know who our customer is or may be, and we know how we will compete, we should be able to know whether the risk is worth the reward.

This shouldn't have to involve accountants and spreadsheets and hours of analysis. What are the number of customers you can capture, and what do you think they will pay for your offerings? As a result, what are the revenues you think you'll gain? How much will it cost you to do that?

Strategy doesn't have to be a squishy subject. It can be strongly focused and hard hitting. Remember what Winston Churchill said, "However beautiful the strategy, you should occasionally look at the results."

Each one of these areas can have clear, measurable metrics to see if you are succeeding or failing so that even the most results oriented among you can see if the time spent on strategy is time well spent.

Think about these questions and address each one with clarity as you plan your next strategy.

Your Business Strategy: By Design or By Default?

You are going to go through life either by design or by default.
~ Rick Warren

It's true. And the same goes for strategy. Many companies I work with tell me, "We don't have a strategy." And I tell them, "Well, the good news is you do. The bad news is you've chosen it by default."

A business strategy is the means by which a business sets out to achieve its desired ends, or objectives. It can be described simply as long-term business planning. You can design that strategy by choosing the desired ends, or you can allow these to happen.

Business strategy is the result of choosing. It's *the result of choices executives make, on where to play and how to win to maximize long-term value.* And often, we don't choose a strategy. We allow a default strategy to happen to us, as opposed to choosing where we want to go.

And in choosing where to play, we choose where not to play. It's important to know how to say, "No."

Think through the fundamental questions you need to ask when creating a business strategy:

- Who is the target customer?
- What is the value proposition for that customer?
- What are the essential capabilities needed to deliver that value proposition?

The target customer is not "everyone." When you hear things like "anyone can use this" or "everyone can benefit from x," run the other way.

And the value proposition needs to be clear. Why is someone going to value parting with cash to use your offering? And how are you going to deliver that value? Not just building it, but selling it?

You can forfeit all these decisions, and let them happen to you by default. That's a strategy. It's just not by design. Let me emphasize: Choosing by default happens when we don't understand the potential of your business.

When we're not sure or can't imagine what we are actually capable of achieving, we continue to run our business on the default setting. We keep doing what we've been doing to try our best to maintain our current performance. I would suggest you can do better.

According to a *Harvard Business Review* article in September 2012 and the Boston Consulting Group: "Strategy usually begins with an assessment of your industry." Your choice of strategic style should begin there as well. Although many industry factors will play into the strategy you actually formulate, you can begin by gaining an understanding of the business environment along the following three dimensions:

- *Predictability:* The extent to which the future of the environment can be forecast, which depends on the degree of complexity and dynamic change.
- *Malleability:* The extent to which the environment can be changed or shaped by the actions of companies individually or collectively.
- *Harshness:* The extent to which an environment's lack of resources—a result of economic or competitive conditions—constrains viability and growth."

Often, we choose strategy by default, because we know the drudgery of the annual strategic planning meeting. You may be one of the many who tire of these off-site strategy meetings, thinking that you spend time with your executive team, peers or reports, and then what comes up is obsolete shortly thereafter, or isn't useful at all. And you're not alone. Why is this?

To produce a sound, high-quality strategic plan requires a senior team *to think well together.* But this isn't easy. It becomes even more challenging–and often impossible–when a team sits down to plan with no structure to support them.

Thinking together is quite different from thinking alone. What usually happens at these meetings is a parade of ideas and that is where they fail. I would suggest something I have used successfully as a method to accomplish this goal.

<u>Six</u> Thinking Hats is a simple, effective, parallel-thinking process that helps people be more productive, focused and mindfully involved. It creates an environment where the team thinks together, rather than individually, harnesses the best thinking of the team on how to choose moving forward, and addresses the job of strategy: deciding where to play to win.

In the times we live in today, a business strategy is *sine qua non*, an essential. So, what's your business and your business strategy? Is it deliberate or is it by default? You can choose which it's going to be.

Here's an illustrative quote from Alice in Wonderland:

> *"Would you tell me, please, which way I ought to go from here? "said Alice to the Cheshire Cat.*
> > *"That depends a good deal on where you want to get to," said the Cat.*
> > *"I don't much care where," said Alice.*
> > *"Then it doesn't matter which way you go," said the Cat.*

And don't eat too many doughnuts.

GOOD REVENUE VS. BAD REVENUE

There used to be an ad on TV–from Toys R Us–with a jingle that contained the chant in the song "I don't want to grow up…" (http://www.youtube.com/watch?v=VJJ-ZLdrTwY)—in the lyrics (refrain?)

Many companies of all sizes sing that song at the end of each month or quarter, as they look for revenue to meet their goals and objectives.

What do I mean?

I call this the "all revenue is good revenue" syndrome. This is the one where we sell things we don't make–or we kind of make. But hey, we need to get a deal, so all revenue is good revenue.

So, what is good revenue and what is bad revenue?

Good revenue is revenue aligned with your company strategy. It's revenue derived from a prospect you've identified in your target market place. Customers in your market place seek few or no changes to your product. And the enhancements they do seek are those you recognize, because other customers and prospects have asked for them. In short, the changes they want fit where you are and where you're going.

On the other hand, bad revenue looks opposed to where you are and where you're headed. It comes from a market segment you don't sell to or rarely sell to. Even if it's from the right market segment, bad revenue results from changes they need you to make to your product or service are ones you've never heard of before.

Or the changes look like they were taken from another offering in your market space, and a prospect is trying to make your product or service solve a problem you never intended to solve. In short, they take you off your track, and you are not aligned.

Unfortunately, the "all revenue is good revenue" rule is a corollary to the rule that states that there are only two problems in business: "not enough sales and everything else"

Yes, it is *true* that we all believe when we hit our numbers that we're successful and we're running a good business. Unfortunately, how we reach our numbers and what we have to deliver, does come with ramifications. When we accept business, we know we can't deliver profitably, or that doesn't help our business, the revenue we gain is bad. When we take business that forces us to modify our product offering for only one customer, and that no one else will buy, the revenue that results are bad revenue.

And if we tell ourselves that others will want it even though there's no evidence that other prospects exist, or if we take business from a big and famous company, and we *have* to do business with them regardless of what they want—all of these issues and many more, cause damage to our business we may not see immediately.

How does this happen?

The pressure to perform becomes exaggerated when we haven't aligned our product with our management, marketing, marketing communications and sales. With business-to-business (B2B), marketing and sales cycles are usually measured in months, and the inability to replace deals easily as quarterly or annual goals approach–deals lost or delayed–create extraordinary pressure to be replaced.

The result: We find ourselves taking on deals that don't exactly fit our investment thesis or product strategy, and rationalizing in one way or another.

First, we all have to understand and agree that there's no perfect product. None. Each has deficits, some very real for any particular prospect or customer. These deficits will surface in any market, against any competition, and can prevent marketing and sales execution.

Second, we need to understand that some, crazy perceived "one offs" may actually have strategic value that translates into game-changing market traction and sales–something the customer sees that we and the rest of the market doesn't yet see. These are, however, rare.

Third, we need to understand that we can better the odds with more defined marketing–product management/marketing, marketing communications, etc., combined with whom we sell to, and attracting that market segment and title. Sales will be better, because sales can sell what's in the bag. These definitions and handoffs are critical, and go way beyond simply agreeing on what a lead is or how qualified a lead is.

Now, we do have another alternative, when faced with the product revenues that we fear are bad revenues. We can say one word: No. That said, I can hear the grumbling already. "Wait just a minute. You don't understand the pressure I'm under. My investors expect me to hit certain numbers." I will lose my job if I can't produce these numbers."

And if you do take the bad revenue? You'll just be delaying the inevitable. You're buying time and worsening the situation in the meantime. This means that when you do hit the wall–and you will if you continue to take bad revenue to hit your numbers–the situation you'll be left with will be worse.

The ability to say, "No" to certain prospects or potential customers is important–maybe even essential–to deliver, long-term, sustainable value and profits. Who loses if you don't say, "no"? Your company and your customers both lose. Your company loses, because of its lack of discipline and focus. Your customers lose, when they eventually realize they're using a version of your product no one else has, thus making it more difficult for you to support, maintain and even enhance it. Saying, "No" is an underestimated capability in marketing and sales processes.

When I was first learning business-to-business sales and marketing, we were all educated in a sales method by Xerox Corporation (later Learning International) called Professional Selling Skills, or PSS. This was one of the first consultative-selling skills methods, complete with open and closed questions that led the prospect to agreement.

Of course, there was a section on objection handling. I still remember all the techniques we were taught to reduce and minimize objections. The back stop to a big objection was to review all the features and benefits that did meet customers' needs that you could deliver and put all of those in comparison with the one you couldn't deliver, making it look very small in the requirements or needs. It didn't always work, but many times, it did.

And as solution selling became more popular and sophisticated with SPIN Selling, Strategic Selling, Solution Selling, and Customer Centric Selling, the techniques to match prospects' needs and minimize objections became more sophisticated and effective.

Marketing played a role then, and does now. The selection of key features and enhancements is essential to meeting prospects' and customers' needs. Product management needs a system that works with customers to communicate what can be added to the enhancement/ feature backlog. This can't be a blackhole. The process needs to be a transparent process to enrich the relationship between the customer, the company and the product/service.

Marketing communications also needs to clearly provide the right awareness, lead generation and sales-support materials so that sales don't stray to prospects outside of the defined market in the need for sales revenue. Not having these processes in place for sales allows them to go where they need to bring in deals, and these can be deals you don't want.

So, remember, there are serious consequences to not saying, "No." Many prospects and customers will thank you for pushing back, and actually respect you for discussing with them the issues of not doing something just for them.

And sometimes you'll still get the deal.

EVERYTHING TO EVERYONE MEANS NOTHING TO NO ONE

I had a meeting a few years back with a successful businesswoman. She had started her for-profit trade organization several years before and had built a $5-million business. Now, she was stuck at this level. She felt she had more to sell her members–books, training, online courses, etc.–and badly wanted to grow her business. She asked me to take a look at her business to see what I would do.

In our initial meeting, I asked her a simple, but important, question: Who is your customer?'

We often overlook this question, or think we know the answer. And often, when I ask a company CEO the question of who is his or her customer, I hear something like "The Fortune 500" or the "Global 2000". (Buzzer please)-WRONG! The Fortune 500 and the Global 2000 are lists. These are not customers.

When I think about customers, I want specifics, like titles, and related demographics–age, gender, income level, likes, dislikes, favorite movies, songs, magazines, restaurants–and the typical type of person that inhabits that customer role. I want to know in detail who they are.

This information is important in B2B marketing, not just B2C marketing. In most B2B sales, the sale is complex. Different people in different roles play various parts in the decision. Know them all.

Market segmentation like this might sound fluffy and academic. But it's critical to building a successful company. Know whom you sell to and why.

Let's look at how Wikipedia, the oracle of knowledge, defines market segmentation:

> "While there may be theoretically 'ideal' market segments, in reality every organization engaged in a market will develop different ways of imagining market segments, and create product differentiation strategies to exploit these segments. The market segmentation and corresponding product differentiation strategy can give a firm a temporary commercial advantage. Most market segmentations are the techniques used to attract the right customer."

If you can identify to whom you sell and why, you can build the right features into your product. (in today's world often referred to as "use cases" and "personas"). You can create the right elements of the service you deliver. You can understand the pricing you can obtain. You can define the sales process and describe the issues and benefits that will meet what various buyers will care about.

In complex, B2B buying cycles, you can have different buyers with various needs. You need to understand them all. And create a Venn diagram where the needs overlap.

Just as thinking you have no competition and assuming that everyone needs your product or service is naïve. Worse still, this approach can damage your business. As with many parts of a business strategy and execution, you need to learn to say, "No."

Even people in your target market are not going to buy your products or services. They may choose to buy your competitor's product or service. They may decide to do things the way they do them today. Or last, they may select apathy and do nothing. Everyone is a not a buyer.

All of this brings me back to the client I mentioned earlier. How do you decide who your customer is? Start with your current customers. What are their patterns? What do they share in terms of size of company (number of employees and revenue) and characteristics of their business. Which ones bring you the most business?

Your products and services will give you other clues. Write out a list of each feature of your product or service. Next to each feature, list the benefits your product or service provide and the advantage of these benefits. Then, make a list of people who have a need that your benefits fulfill.

Look at your selling and processes. Examine the *user buyer,* the person who will use your product or service; the *coach or champion buyer,* who can help you get through the process of the purchase, understand the players, and literally champion your sale; the *economic or financial, buyer,* the person who holds the purse strings; and the *technical buyer* who screens requests for proposals, evaluates the technical suitability of your product or service, and compares your proposal to that of your competitors. There may be even more buyers. Understand the different titles you sell to and match them with these different roles.

Typically, the biggest mistake I have seen in sales happens with the prospect who has pain, the *user buyer.* The sale never goes anywhere, because the user buyer won't take you to others in the organization and therefore, you have no *champion/coach buyer.* This results in a dead end and often blaming the marketing department for lousy leads or the development organization for a product that doesn't sell.

I experienced this first hand at eBillingHub, where I was a founder and CEO, also the leader and sometimes the only salesperson. The person who had the problem with eBilling was typically a billing administrator who never wanted to tell anybody that he or she couldn't get the bills out or that there were mistakes or issues with them. It was only when we reached the VP of Finance or the CFO, the IT director, and the lawyers that we could make the sales case and reach a buying decision.

A great method for focusing on these various roles and aligning the sales messaging comes from Customer Centric Selling, and its Solution Development Prompter. Check out http://smartlemming.com/blog/2009/06/smart-lemming-diary-creating-sales-development-prompters/.

Of course, there are demographics and psychographics and many more ways to complete market segmentation. In any event, it's critical to follow the three rules of market segmentations. They must be:

1. Identifiable
2. Accessible
3. Substantial

Identifiable members of market segments can be enumerated and evaluated. *Accessible* means that members of a market can be reached or impacted by some directed marketing activity. *Substantial* means promising sufficient business to justify the efforts to serve it.

Which brings me back again to the client I mentioned at the beginning.

She ran a trade organization that helped those who managed IT assets for businesses.

Who was her customer? She replied, "Anyone with a PC."

Wow.

Remember: Everyone is not your market

WHY VALUE PROPOSITION IS SO DIFFICULT

Have you ever heard someone say, "Why, of course, what we have to sell has value. I talked to a lot of people, and everyone really wants this. They can't wait."

I heard it again yesterday from a young entrepreneur ready to embark on her startup journey. Her statement elicited memories of two other products everybody thought would be hits—the Apple Watch and Code Name Ginger.

I remember reading in the Tech Section of the Wall Street Journal, when a reporter headlined his article with the question, "What Exactly Is an Apple Watch For?" The article went on to state, "That left Apple executives struggling to define the purpose of the smart watch and wrestling with why a consumer would need or want such a device. Their answer, for now, is a little bit of everything..."

And the Apple Smart watch wouldn't be alone. We all know spectacular new technologies and products that fail. In recent memory, comes Ginger. Do you remember "Code Name Ginger"?

Dean Kamen, a truly great researcher and inventor, had invented a new transportation technology so revolutionary that Steve Jobs of Apple stated, "It's going to be as big as the PC." Jeff Bezos, CEO and founder of Amazon. stated this about Ginger, "You have a product so revolutionary, you'll have no problem selling it. The question is, are people going to be allowed to use it?"

Legendary venture capitalist of Kleiner Perkins, John Doerr, topped it off by stating Ginger would be "More important than the Internet."

Want to guess what Ginger is today? It's the Segway.

Yes, the transportation vehicle you see mall cops using and for guided city tours.

Kamen expected to sell 10,000 units a week by the end of 2002, or half a million a year. In the next six years, Segway sold just 30,000 units, according to Forbes.

So why did this happen we're left to ask? Because creating value proposition is difficult. Here are three, major reasons why:

Technology-Centric. This is probably the most common cause of failure. We think a technology is valuable, because we created it and we see its value. So, we assume that everyone else is like us and should be like us as well, right? We fall in love with our technology/product. And we become very defensive about it. And we rationalize that it will be successful. People, we reason, bought pet rocks too, so they should buy this.

Test, Test, Test. So why do we fail? Often, it's because we don't test our assumptions. We don't go out and ask who we believe are our soon-to-be-customers, if they really want what we're going to build and deliver to the market. It's really that simple. Again, we rationalize with quotes from Steve Jobs or Henry Ford that we don't need to ask customers. (Bad news for most of us: You are not Steve Jobs or Henry Ford). All this while a lot of the new methodologies to deliver technologies, like Agile or Lean, is all about reducing these risks by testing by using the "Build-Measure-Learn" cycle.

Value was not enough to change. Sometimes, we're lucky and sometimes, we're good. Sometimes we're both. If you've successfully created a value, the second part you need to understand is "is it enough" for prospects to change their current behaviors or from their current solutions. Their current solutions don't have to be a direct competitor; they can be indirect. Or they can be apathy or not doing anything. The value and the requirement to change is also based on the level of pain or gain relative to where else they can spend their time or money or both.

There are many others as well, but these tend to be most common. If you want to get your value proposition better, I'd strongly suggest you spend some time reading the book, *Value Proposition Design: How to Create Products and Services Customers Want* by Alexander Osterwalder and Yves

Pigneur. This book is the latest and perhaps, the best thinking so far on creating compelling value.

The last comment on this big subject to think about is this: Value propositions aren't simply communications vehicles. You can't shine a turd. If you've built the value proposition correctly, the marketing communications that sells your value will fall out from it. But it doesn't work the other way around, though many try.

Have a good journey.

The One Thing You Need to Remember about Product-Line Extensions

Remember the old Saturday Night Live fake ad about Shimmer? If you forgot this one, or are too young, watch it here: http://www.nbc.com/saturday-night-live/video/shimmer-floor-wax/n8625?snl=1. "New Shimmer is a floor wax and a dessert topping," states Chevy Chase in the commercial.

And this brings us to the one thing to remember about product-line extensions: One brand cannot be two things. It just can't.

That's because your mind doesn't work that way. And that's why it's funny in the SNL ad. But it's not funny in real business. It's deadly.

Companies spend millions, if not billions, on branding an item, and positioning it correctly in the market and in the minds of buyers. This creates the value of what's called brand equity. This has real value every year, and the value of major brands actually shows up on the balance sheets of real companies that own these brands.

As Al Ries and Jack Trout, the marketing gurus and creators of *Positioning*, said so well many years ago, product line extensions create a short-term win for the extended brand: think beer, Coors and Coors Light. Then the extended brand diminishes and the primary brand is damaged. It's that simple.

Here's an article from Al Ries on the subject in an *Ad Age* from 2009 that explains this effect on a beer brand, Budweiser, and how a line-extension brand can devour a primary brand: http://adage.com/article/al-ries/ries-line-extensions-brand/138797/.

Mr. Ries wrote this about line-extension strategies: "We call line extension the 'hockey-stick effect.' Short term, you get the blade and score a few goals. Long term, you get the shaft." And that's the message.

Here's the one thing to remember about product-line extension: Line extension is a loser's game. It doesn't usually work, but even if it does, it almost always damages the core brand.

When I mention Microsoft or Hertz or IKEA, certain words come to mind that include attributes of a brand, good and bad, and a positioning of the products. These companies invested a lot to get you to think that way.

Simply put, your brand is your promise to your customer. Your brand tells them what they can expect from your products and services, and it differentiates your offering from your competitors. Your brand is derived from who you are, who you want to be and who people perceive you to be. Why waste it or diminish it?

The reality is that managers perceive extensions as a low-cost, low-risk way to meet the needs of various customer segments. Line extensions have been known to satisfy consumers' desires by providing a wide variety of goods under a single brand.

Managers often use extensions as a short-term, competitive weapon to increase a brand's control over limited shelf space or even to get in the bag with their own salesforce in the case of B2B selling.

But for all the perceived benefits, the costs of line extensions are dangerously high. That's because the strategic role of each product becomes muddled when a line is over segmented. Furthermore, a company that extends its line risks undermining brand loyalty.

And here's the killer: Line extensions rarely expand category demand. Most important, the costs of overextension can remain hidden.

When you're devising a new product or service, stop with the line extension. Unless you want a cheap and cheerful solution that will help you in the short term until you find your next job. And enjoy the Shimmer. And maybe you will also enjoy your "AriZona Nachos 'n Cheese Dip"— or is that Ice Tea?

You Have Your Product-Market Fit So, What's Next? Your Pitch-Persona Fit

It's been more than ten years–June 25, 2007 to be exact–since Marc Andreessen coined the term, "product-market fit." In his blog, he stated "Product-market fit means being in a good market with a product that can satisfy that market."

Many people interpret product-market fit as creating a Minimum Viable Product (MVP) that addresses and solves a problem or fills a need that exists. Product-market fit has been the rage since then.

We have had years of building methods, story boards, frameworks, and models–see Eric Ries's *Lean Startup* and Alexander Osterwalder's *Business Model Canvas*–that have helped us divine this essential part of creating and building a successful, product and business."

In short, we're all drinking the Kool-Aid, and without this, we're done. Toast. Finito. Even the big kahuna himself, Marc Andreessen, tells us: "The life of any startup can be divided into two parts–before product-market fit and after product-market fit."

So, listen up. I'm no Marc Andreessen. I've never developed or worked on a product as significant as Mosaic. I didn't coin terms like "software is eating the world." I'm not a multi-billionaire. And I've never had my big toes displayed on *Time* magazine. (See Feb.19, 1996 "*The Golden Geeks.*")

With that clear differentiation between Marc and me out of the way, let me state that there is an important next step after product-market fit that may be as critical as the product-market fit. It's called the "pitch-persona Fit".

"What is this?" you might ask.

Let's break it down starting with the word, "persona." There is this thing called the customer. I prefer prospect since they haven't purchased anything yet, but let's not quibble and keep it at customer for now. He or she lives inside the market.

And if you don't know whom I mean specifically, whom that customer is, you are lost. In short, per HubSpot, "A buyer persona is a semi-fictional representation of your ideal customer, based on market research and real data about your existing customers. When creating your buyer persona(s), consider including customer demographics, behavior patterns, motivations, and goals. The more detailed you are, the better."

By the way, I had a mentor who used to say when people complained about customers complaining or being difficult, "We tried it (the business) for a while without any customers and that was fun, but then we wanted to get paid."

I have written more on the topic of pitching later in this book. See "The Art of the Pitch". Pitching is persuasion distilled into a presentation. It's defined as "a line of talk that attempts to persuade someone or something, with a planned sales-presentation strategy of a product or service designed to initiate and close a sale of the product or service." At its essence, it's storytelling.

Remember that stories beat facts. The story you tell may, however, be different for each persona. And that's where you need the "fit" between the two.

And you need to understand the foundational elements of each of your pitches and use pieces and parts of them for your pitches to the right personas. The pitch you give your prospect is not what you give your investors. And that's different from what's used at a company meeting. But let's not stray too far.

Here's a real-life example. When I was the CEO of eBillingHub, we had three customers. Not atypical of a B2B complex sale. In the early days, we didn't have much traction, because we tried to sell to the person who had the billing problem, the billing manager.

They would love to see demos and hear how it could help them solve the problems of electronic billing. But we realized that they couldn't buy anything. They were what I called "Seymours." They always wanted to "See More." And they didn't buy. But they were important to the sale.

We also identified IT persons as influencers. Sometimes, they could stop the sales for a number of reasons like integration, security, etc. Or they would tell management they could build something in house to save money. So, they could say, "No," but not "Yes." But, they had a seat at the table. And they needed to be sold.

Finally, there was the CFO or VP of Finance. Many times, they didn't understand the day-to-day issues of the billing managers and their staffs, or didn't know as ebilling volumes grew. But they did care about cash flow, collections and end-of-year distributions to partners.

We had three, different personas. And one product. And a set of product features and benefits. And we needed to get the 'fit" right between the pitch for each persona. If we sold the CFO on entering the correct syntax to reduce billing errors, it was interesting but not compelling. But if we told them how the product would reduce days sales outstanding, (DSO), they perked up.

In short, we had "product-market fit,"' and we knew it. But the business didn't accelerate until we solved the "pitch-persona fit".

So, what's next in your new-product or startup journey? If you have the "Product Market Fit," then make it actionable with the "Pitch Persona Fit."

Four Lessons I Learned as a Young Product Manager That Still Guide Me Today

Early in my career, I worked with a great fellow product manager, Greg Strouse, who became a lifelong friend. As both our careers progressed, Greg used to tell me that no matter what new jobs or roles we took on, we could always go back and be product managers and that it would be fun.

I still agree with that thought in many ways, because I don't think I ever stopped thinking of myself as a product manager, no matter what role I've actually played in a company.

When I worked with Greg in the early days of the software market, almost 30 years ago, I had the opportunity to work on several, enterprise software products, all with different market challenges and in different product life cycles.

We had the classic Boston Consulting Group/BCG "cash-cow" products, questions, markets, and stars, as well as a few dogs. Owning and managing a portfolio of these products formed many of the lessons I learned and applied to building other products, programs, and even companies.

One product in particular, AutoMate, an early-stage enterprise, data-center automation product and later market leader, taught me a lot of about product go-to-market strategies. Here are four lessons I learned:

1. **Doman expertise is overrated.** As a young product marketer, my job was to assure profitable, top-line revenue growth. I needed

to find other products that would form a suite of high-growth (defined as better than a compound, annual growth rate of 35 percent) offerings. Internally, we also competed for resources with other product groups and if we couldn't show the need for these resources, we would be left behind. So, we were competing internally and externally.

Then, the automated-operations market came along, and changed everything. I had worked in factory automation at EATON Cutler-Hammer, and then at Gulf & Western/Eagle Signal Controls businesses straight out of college as a sales engineer. I knew the pluses and minuses of marketing automation, and "unattended" and "lights out' messaging in a different marketplace. To sell this to information technology people, however, would be different, yet the same.

Lesson: Use your experiences from other market places, verticals, segments, and hire people who have these experiences.

If I had simply worked in the information-technology industry, I wouldn't have had the advantages I brought to the market. This goes for hiring for domain expertise. It's neither always necessary nor good. Sometimes, having different market experiences is key to having competitive advantages.

So, stop hiring someone who comes from some other company you like or whom you think are better just because of their domain expertise. They may not be right, and they may attach boundaries around what's possible that actually constrain your capabilities.

Again, I was able to use the lessons from the factory-automation marketplace and apply them successfully to the data center automation market. It was like I had seen the movie already and knew the outcome. It was "Groundhog Day" in many ways, and I knew how the day would play out. Competitive advantage may not come from where you expect or from obvious places.

2. **Differentiate. Don't just catch up.** For a variety of reasons, our product was behind in the market when we launched. We were in the classic Losers quadrant of the Gartner Magic Quadrant. We had our work cut out for us and even knew what we had to do to win. See Number 1 above.

We, as all companies do, had a decision to make: Where do we put our resources? If we didn't start winning revenue and customers, the company would place its bets on other markets and with other internal teams.

We decided to bet on differentiating functionality, or something that moves a product ahead, rather than catching up on base functionality, something a prospect already expects to receive in a product.

This was a huge risk for us. Would the differentiation be valuable enough to overcome the base functionality that competitors had? And if we were successful, what would we do next? Would we further extend the differentiation to then go back and use the advantage to catch up?

These were all strategic, product questions we had to play out as we tried to decide how best to play the chess game of product marketing.

We bet big on the differentiating feature, a capability that allowed our product to integrate a variety of existing tools and pieces of data. This did, in fact, have enough value to drives sales and give us time to catch up with base functions.

Different was better. This also put us in the Leaders quadrant of the next Gartner Magic Quadrant.

Let me be clear. That's not to say this works every time. It was a bet that we won. If the differentiation hadn't had such really significant value, we probably would have lost. But as Eminem sang, "Look, if you had one shot, one opportunity to seize everything you ever wanted, one moment, would you capture it or just let it slip?"

We captured it. Big time. And for years, the product became one of the market leaders and largest revenue producers of the company.

3. **Poison the salesforce one at a time.** This is for B2B sales geeks. A sales force is your first customer. If your product doesn't fit into the salespeople's bag, if you can't show them how to make money with your product, compared to other things, they won't sell your product. They can sell to make their numbers, but your

product will never get out of their sales bag. Even with the best, most differentiated product, you will lose.

You need your sales force to get to your customer. To sell them. And *how* you sell them is important.

Just as when you do a soft launch or a beta test with early customers, you need to do the same with your sales team. In the words of an old friend, Paul Johnson, you need to *poison* them one at a time. Just what does this mean?

Most likely, the salespeople who can pay attention to your new product at launch time are those who aren't making their numbers, who are willing to take a risk on something new, because they aren't selling what's available now.

And about those who are making their numbers or blowing them out, or are selling other stuff successfully, the question is: Why would they sell something new? You need to get in their bag. Just like customer segmentation, target the salespeople you want to sell your product. Work with them closely. Make them successful. Make them referenceable salespersons about whom other salespeople think, "Hey, they're making money selling 'X' product; I'll give it a shot."

Poison them. One at a time.

4. **Go wide not deep**. Everyone loves the idea and the reality of full-featured, robust capabilities in a product. But in many cases, you can't, or shouldn't, develop these capabilities. I like to think the best way to do most features is to define the minimum set of functionalities that demonstrates the capability. No more or less.

Think of it as Revision 1 of the feature. You'll get more chances to build it out. And just as a Minimum Viable Product (MVP) has only those core features that allow the product to be deployed and no more, you need to think of individual features that same way.

Start small, and then get feedback. Test *sale-ability* of the function or feature; get prospect and customer feedback. If you build it out all the way in the first release, you've poured too many resources in one area. That's too big a risk with little market feedback.

Going back to my earlier example in section Number 2 of this chapter, when we released that key differentiating feature, we didn't develop a lot of new functionality; we used existing code without modifying it from another product we sold. And once it drove sales, we refined it.

If we'd spent the time to develop the code from scratch and made it picture perfect, and the idea had failed, we would have spent a lot more money and would have been even further behind.

I could easily write dozens more lessons from my earlier job that still guide me today.

It was a great experience being a young product manager at a company with multiple products in different lifecycles, but overall in hyper-growth mode. I learned a lot that I continue to apply through my career.

Different Beats Better

W e're better. We're different.

At times, the difference between being different or better seems irrelevant. It can even be dismissed. Or it may even be too simple to discuss.

But, it's certainly worth discussing. Are your company, products, and services different or are they better? Can they be both? Should they be both?

These two adjectives–different and better–have a marked impact on what you decide you want to be and they have strategic implications for how you go to market.

They are also critical to what we sell to our customers. Our basic value proposition is based on whether we feel we are better or different or both.

Let's start with some definitions. What does better *mean?*

Our friends at *Merriam Webster* define the word, better, like this: "higher in quality; more skillful; more attractive, appealing, effective, useful, etc."

Examples include: "Her second book is *better* than her first one; this one is *no better* than that one; she's a *better* golfer than I am."

And different? What does different mean? *Merriam Webster* tells us that it means "not of the same kind: partly or totally unlike; not the same."

Cost. Differentiation. Focus. Choose one. With these definitions of better and different as a background, let's look to Michael Porter, an expert in competition and competitive advantage, to see what he says is important when businesses compete. He's the author of 18 books, including *Competitive Strategy*, and 125 articles.

In *Competitive Strategy*, Professor Porter wrote that a company's strategy should target either <u>cost leadership</u>, <u>differentiation</u>, or <u>focus</u>. These terms are known as Porter's three, generic strategies that can be applied to any size or form of business.

Porter claims that a company must only choose *one* of the three or risk wasting precious resources. Some businesses attempt to adopt all three strategies of cost leadership, differentiation and niche (focus). A business adopting all three strategies is known as "stuck in the middle." Such a business has no clear business strategy and is attempting to be everything to everyone.

This approach is likely to increase running costs and cause confusion, because it's difficult to please all sectors of a market. Middle of the road businesses usually perform the worst in their industries, because they don't concentrate on one, single business strength.

What's interesting is that Porter never mentions "better" as a strategy, as in "*do what your competition does and do it better.*" Why? Because this is not a sustainable, competitive advantage. It's temporary. Being better simply doesn't last. Being different does.

And what Porter calls "focus" is sometimes called "segmentation." Good examples of focus are Rolls Royce and Bentley cars, both of which are focused on high-end car buyers with premium cars. And what is that really, but another form of difference?

Thus, we're left with different vs. cost. And Porter's thoughts on that? He emphasizes that it may be difficult to sustain cost leadership in the long run. So that leaves us with only one path forward: different.

Twenty-five years later, *Blue Ocean Strategy* was published by W. Chan Kim and Renée Mauborgne, Professors at INSEAD and Co-Directors of the INSEAD Blue Ocean Strategy Institute. Based on a study of 150 strategic moves spanning more than 100 years and 30 industries, Kim and Mauborgne show that companies can succeed not by battling competitors, but rather by creating "blue oceans" of uncontested, market space.

This metaphor exemplifies that you shouldn't compete in a red ocean, because that represents what already exists today. Why a blue ocean? Simply this: It's not about being better. It's about being different.

As a young product manager, I was in charge of an early-stage product, Automate/MVS, in a new, emerging marketplace. The product was late to market, with fewer features than the competition, and was priced incorrectly among many other issues with the offering. In short, it was dead on arrival when it launched.

Although there were many decisions to be made about how to move ahead with the product, or whether to move ahead at all, we decided on one important thing: To be different.

We purposefully didn't try to catch up on the feature list with our competition, but instead, we moved ahead with functionality that was totally a cut above in the marketplace. We felt this was sufficient to gain customers. It was a gamble and it worked. Being different paid off and the product not only became a leader in its space, but also excelled as one of the most successful software products of its time.

Think Different(ly). Grammar aside, and with respect to Apple, being able to think differently is a basic definition of innovation. It's also a definition of how to be smart about your business. To stay relevant, to stay current, to stay competitive, you have to be different.

Look at popular culture. How does a pop star like Madonna sell music, when she's more than 58 years old? She's always different. Yes, there's always a thread of familiarity, and you know what you're going to get when you listen to her music or go to her show. But you also know you're going to be surprised, because she's going to do something that's, well, different.

And to be heard in the crowded, noisy market place we all compete in, how are prospects going to know who you are and what you do? By being better? No one says, "Oh, XYZ Corporation, they're the ones that make that better stuff."

Yet, we hold endless meetings and discussions about how we can build something better. But customers buy different, not better. They remember different, not better.

So, think about yourself, your products and services, and your company, and ask, "Why are we different?" By being different, you may surprise yourself over how much better you really are.

THERE ARE ONLY TWO PROBLEMS IN BUSINESS

As a consultant, I'm often asked to help a company with its strategy. When I respond, the company is usually suffering with these symptoms:

1. Low/flat sales.
2. Technology is searching for a problem that results in low/flat sales.
3. They had success with an initial set of customers, and that has now gone away, resulting in low/flat sales.

See the pattern?

Years ago, I worked for a gentleman named Lee Ehrlichmann, who used to say, "There are only two problems in business: not enough sales and everything else." Not sure if Lee was the first to come up with that, but I can say that the number-one reason companies engage me or my company, ENTRA, is that their business has hit a roadblock and they want to get it back on the right track for growth. And they need a strategy.

Let's start there. What, exactly, is a strategy? Well, one way to think of strategy is in terms of a three-legged stool:

- Where are we/you now? (Strengths/Weaknesses),
- Where do we/you want to go? (Opportunities/Threats), and
- How do we/you get there?

44

This seems so simple, almost childlike to the point that the questions are often dismissed or ignored. Isn't there some methodology? Some systems folks used to derive their strategy that results in a winning formula? As if someone could divine how to win football games or elections, just repeat it, and guarantee the outcome.

Often folks are looking for a tag line, or some magic pixie dust that they want to attach their business to, some kind of messaging or set of words to some emerging category like *cloud* or *SaaS*. They then think that the business will miraculously start growing in sales and revenue, that all the employees and investors will be happy, and that everyone will be successful and rich. And all their friends will say, "You worked there? WOW!" And future readers of your resume will say, "You must be successful, because you worked at X company."

This is what I call the Fiddler-on-the-Roof phenomenon: Because you're rich, they think you know it all. But contrary to all this is that strategy is hard work. It's not a tagline. And it's not simply news jacking, or attaching yourself to the latest trend. It's much more.

I agree with the well-known marketing experts and authors, Al Ries and Jack Trout. In their book *Bottom Up Marketing*, they tell us: *All great strategy comes from tactics.* It derives from their work in *Marketing Warfare*. The premise is simple and starts in the field and in sales. Find the repeatable, go-to-market pattern in the sales process. Extrapolate from that and simplify it for marketing messaging.

Ries and Trout argue for the bottom-up approach, because a deep knowledge of tactics effectively used in the field is needed to formulate a strategy that can achieve tactical objectives. More specifically, Ries and Trout argue that the sole purpose of strategy is to put forces in motion to overpower the competitor at the point of contact using the principle of force.

On the military battlefield, this means having more soldiers or forces at the point of battle. On the marketing battlefield, it means overpowering the competitor in a specific position in the mind of the customer.

Ries and Trout further explain that a good strategy doesn't depend on brilliant tactics. Even mediocre tactics are usually sufficient for a good strategy. Even the best possible tactics are unlikely to compensate for a poor strategy. In marketing, advertising may be considered tactics, and many managers falsely assume that success depends almost entirely on the quality of an advertising campaign.

If a strategy requires top-notch tactics to win the battle, Ries and Trout maintain that such a strategy is unsound, because tactical brilliance is rare. Any strategy should take into account the probable response of a competitor. The best way to protect against a response is to attack the weakness in the leading competitor's strength so that the leader can't respond without giving up its strength.

To support the argument of a bottom-up strategy, Ries and Trout point out that many large companies incorrectly believe that they can do anything if they simply allocate enough resources to the job. History shows otherwise. Just recall the failed attempts of Exxon's entry into office systems and Mobil's acquisition of Montgomery Ward.

Such diversions shift resources away from the point of battle where they're needed. This is one of the dangers that you can be avoid with a bottom-up strategy based on what can be accomplished at the tactical level.

The lesson here? Yes, strategy meetings are important. And yes, you should have strategy sessions to get everyone on the same page about messaging and resource allocation. But real strategy happens at the field level, belly to belly with the prospect or customer. And seeing and hearing the pattern there will lead you to the magic pixie dust you desire.

Just one word of caution. As a result of the information above, you may be tempted to listen only to your sales reps to derive a bottom-up strategy. Most likely, that would be a mistake.

Remember that you're looking for patterns, not single incidents of successful tactics. More important, sales are not a market-research tool. And sales are not your strategic divining rod. Sales persons' feedback as to what's working and what's not is colored by their coin operated incentives. Also, the focus of sales people is on individual customers versus a market.

This is as it should be, because strategy isn't a sales concern. Even your head of sales is not necessarily going to see or hear the pattern.

They're after results in revenue, and they don't pull the camera back to see the whole picture. It's not their job and it's generally not how they are wired.

Now get your butt out there and see for yourself. Ask questions. *Why* is a good one to start with.

Of Washing Machines and Dryers: Why the Customer Isn't Always King

One of my favorite lectures I give to my B2B Marketing class is understanding customers versus prospects. It's drilled into our heads that we must listen to the customer and that the customer is king. Some of this is true. But we also need to listen to prospects–those who have yet to purchase. Or those who didn't purchase.

Prospects have a message to tell us, especially if we're interested in growing our business, and we're in the early stages of the product life cycle. Here's an example of what I mean: Think back to when you last purchased your washer and dryer. You probably didn't go out and plop down $2,000 on the latest and greatest washer and dryer, because you felt the need to move to the latest technology or to the coolest, newest features.

Many of us purchase a washer and dryer only when one fails us and it doesn't make sense to repair it. And so, the customer's journey, or in this case, the prospect's journey begins.

If you're like most of us, your use of your existing washing machine is fairly routine. You load clothes and press wash. You take out the clothes, put them in the dryer, hit the right setting, and press dry, or something similar.

It's not a particularly complicated process. And if you're like many of us, you have an older pair of machines where there are not a lot of choices. And that's good, because washing and drying clothes is not a valuable use of your time.

Now, back to our broken machines and the need for new ones. You might head to Lowes, Best Buy, or maybe, to your favorite, local appliance store. And there they appear. The coolest, newest washers and dryers. You're caught up with front loaders and top loaders with no beater bar and stainless-steel insides with loads of capacity for the largest comforter you could ever imagine.

These machines are amazing. They look like '57 Cadillac's with fins! They have a myriad of buttons and controls to wash stuff to "scare away" allergies with steam. They come with buttons to wash now, dry later, or to clean your clothes fast, or even to wash, when you please.

You'll even find washers to clean some clothes without having to take them to the dry cleaners. Likewise, dryers have all kinds of cool, new buttons: Some dryers automatically turn off to prevent clothes from over drying and shrinking. And some use steam to refresh an outfit you've worn already, to relax wrinkles and to remove odors so you don't have to rewash it.

And some promise to dry in no time. I like the ones with the sneakers insert to stop that noise of tumbling tennis shoes in your dryer. It's fantastic what you can do.

And did I forget the wonderful add-ons you can buy? My favorite item is the pedestal that makes sure you have extra storage right below your washer and dryer or to make sure your front loaders are the at the right level to avoid your having to stoop over to load them. And for a mere $250 per unit–$500 for both–these deluxe, matching pieces of sheet metal are yours.

And so, you look and decide. Right down to the color. Who wants white anymore? Green, black, blue, and even pink are available. You plop down your $2,000 or $2,500, take delivery, and you're truly excited that you have these cool-looking, full-featured units.

And what do you do with your new washer and dryer? Well, if you're like most folks, you still just press wash and then dry. And what about all those features you couldn't do without? You really wanted them. And you saw their value. But you use the new machines just like the old ones.

Now, for some takeaways: You aren't unusual. In one circumstance, you're a customer. If a product manager asked you what you wanted, you'd probably say, "I'm happy. I press wash or dry, the thing does its stuff, and it works."

But as a prospect, you wanted so much more. As a matter of fact, you *needed*, not just wanted, so much more. Now, I appreciate that some of you are more logical, and this example may not include you or the way you do things. But some time in your life you exhibit the same behaviors.

And it's important for those of us who build features into new products to understand this. To simply go back to the customer base and build the next incremental feature, or define our next epic, or story, or theme isn't enough. We need to look through the lens of the persona or *whom* this is for. When we do product-release planning, we need to ask how much of this product is for the prospect, the (market, versus competition, strategy)–versus the customer(existing revenues, strategy, etc.). Early in my career, I was the product manager for a successful product. It became so, because we added a feature that was ground breaking and highly valued by prospects. Even though the product had less functionality than the competition, we were able to surpass the competition and become the leader in the market.

There was just one problem. No one used the new feature. That's right. Everyone had to have it, but no one used it. About two years after our product release, a customer-service person asked me if we needed to support it anymore because no one used it. He suggested eliminating the feature. He was simply listening to the customer, not the prospect.

Every product release has catch-up, keep-up, and leg-up features. You can find a thousand ways to think about what they are and how to prioritize them. Just make sure you don't forget the mix between prospect and customer and be explicit about what you're emphasizing in your next release.

How to Stand Out in a Noisy Market: Defeating the "Me Too"

Years ago, Jack Trout and Al Ries wrote a book called *Positioning*. It was based on an article they had written in *Advertising Age* in 1969, on the same issue. Much of what Ries and Trout wrote remains true today, despite significant changes in the marketing business.

Companies still struggle with the same issue: How do I stand out in a noisy market, when everybody sounds the same? This is where positioning comes in.

Positioning, the book, is about how to define your product or entity in an optimal way to differentiate them from competitors and to drive preferential purchase or use. Ries and Trout argue that positioning has become especially critical for marketers as our society has become over-burdened with communications and advertisements.

Their book drives home the point that the only reality that matters is the perception of your customers and prospects. Their world view and interpretation of your product counts, not yours.

When I hear that it was really crowded at the XYZ tradeshow, and every exhibitor sounded the same, I think, "What is their positioning?"

Let's return to the definition of Ries and Trout, still valuable over 30 years since they wrote their book. "Positioning is how you differentiate yourself in the mind of the prospect."

I like to think of it as the B2B equivalent of branding. Branding for me still has a B2C sound and feel, but it is used in the B2B world.

Positioning is defining the meaning of an offering to positively differentiate it from the competition and drive preferential purchase, trial, or use.

Positioning is about reaching and filling a vacant spot in the mind of the prospective customer, decision maker, end-user, et al. And positioning can apply to anything—a product, company, service, person, etc.

Here are some rules about positioning:

Narrow Your Target. The more narrowly defined your target the better. We can't successfully communicate, position, or understand prospects' minds without first segmenting the market and focusing on a narrower set.

What's clear here is that going deep and wide is not your friend. Everything to everyone means nothing to no one. If you can do it all with your product, don't. It's a mistake if you do. Focusing and narrowing are your friends. Be good at something versus trying to be good at everything.

Focus on the prospect, not the product. To select your message, look for the solution to your problem not inside the product, not inside your own mind, but inside the prospect's mind. Concentrate on the perceptions of the prospect, not the qualities or reality of the product.

In short, you need to walk in the shoes of your prospect. No one cares what you think. Only your prospect matters. You don't buy anything. Your prospect does. Know how prospects perceive the problem your product is solving and the benefit it provides. This is what I call outward-in thinking from the prospect to your product, not the other way around.

Oversimplify. In an increasingly over communicated society, you're lucky if people can remember one message and associate it with your product. Less is more. Oversimplify and stick to a single message.

Think about how many emails you get in a day. The average is 121. And we spend about 1 to 2 seconds reading the subject line before deciding what to do with it. If you still read snail mail, think about the process of opening your mailbox when you retrieve your mail and how you sort it. It's estimated that you spend about 2 to 3 seconds per piece of mail.

No matter how we are communicated with, the average adult's attention span is down to just 8 seconds. That's less than that of a goldfish. According to Harvard psychologist, Dr. George A. Miller, the average human mind cannot deal with more than 7 units at a time. That's why 7 is a popular number for lists that have to be remembered.

If you don't simplify, you won't even have a chance to get heard. Think of seven-digit phone numbers, the Seven Wonders of the World, seven-card stud, Snow White and the Seven Dwarfs.

Be first. The best way to get into a person's mind is to be first. What's the tallest mountain in the world? Mount Everest at 29,029 feet. What's the second tallest? People know Charles Lindbergh was the first man to fly across the Atlantic. How about the second person?

Find a position in the prospect's mind that you can be first in. It's better to be a big fish in a small pond than to be a small fish in a big pond. Create a category you can win in. Define the category differently so that you are the biggest, best, and most awesome. You have to be number 1 or number 2.

Now, that doesn't mean being first to market. Pioneers often get the arrows in their backs. This means first in the minds of your prospects. There is a difference.

Make your first impression count. You never get a second chance with a product, company, or even as a person to make a first impression. When two people meet and end up falling in love, it requires an open window, or vacant spot, and both individuals being receptive to the idea. The same type of situation has to occur when you position a product.

You also have to understand how prospects think. Many companies want to define what the prospects think of their companies without even finding out first, what prospects think of them now! They want to just will them to think of them the way they believe they should. Then, they have some marketing leader run a program to change prospects' minds. If only it were that easy.

The first step is to understand that you already have a position in the prospect's mind. Understand that first. And remember that prospects, like people, reject incongruent information. If your positioning strategy involves changing what people already think, you'll have a difficult time.

The best strategies are congruent with what people already think. The mind accepts only what matches prior knowledge or experience. McDonald's as a gourmet steak alternative to Morton's? Not a chance.

The book, *Positioning*, is a classic. If you haven't read it, I encourage you to. If you read it years ago, it's worth a reread. Even though many examples are dated, it's still relevant in today's me-too world.

I Hate Trade Shows. There, I Said It.

You, the marketing professional, may hate one of the top vehicles in your profession. Nonetheless, it's the beginning of the year and last fall, you did your budget. You set forth your strategy and supported it with tactics that boil down to specific marketing activities, like a trade show. Maybe a national trade show. Maybe a regional trade show. Maybe your company goes to the same shows every year.

Maybe, you've decided to attend a new one to see what happens. Perhaps, you've even surveyed your sales teams and asked them what trade shows they feel you should attend. Who knows, but you are going to spend the time and money. Trade shows are in your marketing mix.

And the reason why? Well, someone will inevitably state, "What will it look like if we aren't there?"

Well, despite my aversion to trade shows, they do have a purpose and can be effective. And to be clear, my perspective comes mainly from the B2B technology business. That may limit my perspectives and opinions relative to other B2B or B2C trade-show events. With these statements out of the way, let's chat a little bit about trade shows.

Let me say it again. I hate trade shows. Mostly. Trade shows have changed in the 30 years I have been involved in planning and executing them. They've gone from a *lead-generation* vehicle to an *awareness* vehicle. I state this, because I see a lot of suspects being collected in scanned attendee badges or business cards in a fish bowl. But I don't see a lot of qualified leads, business transactions advancing, or progressing deals. I certainly don't see deals being done.

The trade show has become a physical ad that represents an image, a branding and positioning, of your company to a wide variety of prospects. Yes indeed, leads are collected. Yes, the fish bowl is alive and well.

Conversations start with people and their companies that are interested. And yes, demonstrations take place to help show off the capabilities for some of the most interested. This is all goodness. But here are some disturbing facts.

Shows are expensive. Especially for small businesses and start-ups. The smallest space you can typically get is a 10-foot x 10-foot space. The average square-foot cost for exhibits is about $23. Therefore, if you're planning a 10 x 10 booth (100 square feet) your costs should be $23 x 100, or $2,300.

And figure your total trade-show cost will be three times the cost of the exhibit space. That's about $7,000. What would that include? Well, we need people to staff the booth. That's a minimum of 2, most likely 3 sales people. Don't even say you could get by with one, because that's just plain silly. You'd be wasting your money.

And, it's $2,000 per person for airfare, hotel, meals, etc. That's another $6,000. People do have to take breaks, and you do want to check out the other exhibitors from a competitive perspective, and meet with the press, analysts, et al.

And remember, if you want to have a prayer at getting the right prospects to your booth, consider this: You'll probably have a 10-foot x10-foot exhibit space in the back of the third floor of the exhibit hall. That's because most shows do placement based on years of loyalty. Those who have exhibited at the show every year will have the opportunity both to pay more and to get better show positions.

All of which means that you must promote your attendance to the attendees. That's prior to the show beginning; that's activities during the show; and maybe most important, after the show with follow up with whom you met and with those you didn't. These things can run about 19 percent of your costs.

Sure, you don't have to do them. But then, how are you actually translating the value of the show? Isn't it about driving business? The marketing aspects are expensive and shouldn't be overlooked. And then, there are things you can sponsor, which cost money like coffee breaks, hospitality rooms, and the like.

Plus, you'll have your own specialty-advertising items like give-aways, often called "specialty advertising" or commonly referred to as "tchotchkes." And they need to be purchased, shipped, and handed out. And they need to be different and underscore your message of "don't forget." In short, there are lots of marketing expenses. Lots.

We didn't even discuss the cost of creating the booth. Even the cheap and cheerful Skyline pop up display will cost you $5,000 to $10,000 for the creation and purchase. Tour graphics will need to be updated. Now if you need something for a larger space, that means getting it designed and built, and shipped and stored, when you are not using it. And often, it must be assembled by local trade-show builders.

I could go on. In short, it ain't cheap. And if you don't plan and prepare, if you don't schedule meetings in advance and work leads afterwards, it's a lot of money with very little results.

How much did exhibitors spend on average in 2010 per face-to-face meeting at their exhibit? $276 according to Exhibit Surveys Inc. data reported in April 2011 by Exhibitor Magazine. How much did they spend per attendee who entered their exhibit? $189 according to the same source.

And a Marketo study in 2010 tells us that the cost of a lead for other sources looks like this:

- Paid webinar: $68.50
- PPC (Pay Per Click): $158.10
- Email Blast: $34.65.

Other forms are all cheaper. SEO, Blogs, and many other kinds of inbound marketing are particularly less expensive. Hubspot claims that in 2011, the average cost per lead for outbound dominated businesses was $373, while inbound businesses reported their leads cost on average $143.

And specifically, they stated that *Trade Shows were most frequently reported as more expensive than average.* So, do yourself a favor and check out the recommendations that follow.

Here are some common-sense ways to make the most out of your trade-show planning and experience: Think of a show in three stages: Pre, During, and Post.

Pre. The more you prepare for the event the better the event will be. For example, call your best prospects and customers and arrange to meet them at the show, if they're attending the show. Set up meetings with reporters and analysts at the show. Do a pre-show mailing to tell your customers and prospects that you'll be there. And make sure your mailing has a call to action to get them to see you at your booth. Of course, make sure you have a theme and message and get all your booth materials ready to be shipped. For goodness sake, don't take it to the airport and check it in! And make sure everyone knows who is working the booth, and when and what to wear.

During. There is so much to be done during a show, but I have some strong suggestions: Stand. Don't sit; ask questions of those stopping by; don't go right into your pitch. Who knows whom you're talking to? No food, please; collect leads with a scoring mechanism for later; make sure your giveaway has something to do with the message of your business. Anyone will show up for a free T-Shirt or a magician act. And don't give them any paper like a brochure. They'll just throw it away, and that wastes money. Finally, assign someone to do competitive intelligence. Always good to hear and see what your competition is doing. One of the best places to do that is at a trade show.

Post. Follow-up. You just spent a boatload of time and money. Don't let the contacts you've made go to waste, because you're tired and can't find the time to follow up. Following up is where the value is! And have a post-show meeting, please. And not just about how you could make the show better. Talk about your sales pitch. What worked? What didn't?

If you can't do at least some of these pre, during, and post activities, then don't go.

Often, the scariest part of *why* you should participate in a particular trade show is the response: "What would it look like, if we're not there." That's not a reason.

Think through which ones you feel you can attend and do them right. Then, maybe you can even convince me to stop by your booth.

THREE REASONS WHY YOU NEED TO PRACTICE IN BUSINESS

S o, how was practice today? What's that you say? You don't play a sport or an instrument? I know. I was talking about practice, as in business. What's that? You don't practice in your business? Well, maybe you should.

It amazes me that we don't practice our businesses. We've all heard the expression, "practice makes perfect," a million times. Yet, we think of it in a limited sense and don't apply it to our business lives.

And for good reason. You may have several objections to the idea of "business practice" specifically. You might say:

- I don't need to practice in my business. I'm proficient already.
- I don't have time to practice in my business.
- I don't know how to practice in my business.

I understand. These are all reasonable objections. But it may help to first examine what practice is by checking out the definition of the term, practice:

- Repetition of an activity to improve a skill. *"He will need lots of practice with the lines before he performs them."*
- The ongoing pursuit of a craft or profession,

I would add the notion of preparation when thinking about practicing. Many forms of preparation are indeed equivalent to practice in a business context. When it comes to business, practice can involve studying best practices, seeking guidance from mentors and coaches, practicing a difficult conversation with a trusted advisor, attending a webinar, or reading an eBook about key subjects in your profession or that affect your job. These are all ways to practice and prepare in business.

These definitions should help us address the concept of practicing in business. Let's start by addressing the objection, "I don't need to practice in my business"

Did you play basketball in high school? About 535,000 boys and 436,000 girls in the United States alone play basketball every year. Of that, 1 out of 12,114 women will get to the WNBA and 1 out of 8, 926 men will play in the NBA.

In short, they will have practiced a lot, have played many games, and will have practiced 2 to 2.5 hours a day when they didn't have a game.

Think about it. What do professional football teams do each and every week? They practice for the game on Sunday. The game could last a few hours. What does a symphony orchestra do during the week before a concert performance? These elite musicians are found practicing. It's not unusual to have two full days, each with 2 or 3 hours of rehearsal sessions in them, before a concert or series of concerts. Each concert will also have an additional *balance rehearsal* of up to three hours in the afternoon before an evening concert later that day.

Like professional athletes, these musicians are at the top of their forms. As of 2007, there were 117 U.S. orchestras with annual budgets of $2.5 million or more. If you play clarinet or trumpet that may give you the opportunity to play at 250 to 400 positions in the United States if someone retires or otherwise vacates a seat. More, of course, for string positions but still not that many. Like the professional athlete, to get here you must be at the top of your game in all aspects. And these musicians practice continually.

When we learn a new skill, whether it's programming in Ruby on Rails, providing customer support over the phone, playing chess, or doing a cartwheel, we're changing how our brain is wired on a deep level. Science has shown us that the brain is incredibly plastic. This means the brain does not harden at age 25 and stay solid for the rest of our lives.

Whereas certain things, especially language, are more easily learned by children than adults, we have plenty of evidence that even older adults can see real transformations in their neurocircuitry. That's right. There's a true, physical benefit to practice: Practicing skills over time causes neural pathways to work better in unison.

So first of all, accept that no matter how good you are and how well educated you are or both, *you need to practice.* We all do. It's about improving and learning.

And the best of the best in any profession does it, and so should you.

Let's address time. None of us has as much time as we want. We can't fit in what needs to be done, let alone what we want to get done. So now you want me to practice? Ugh!

So how much is enough?

Dr. K. Anders Ericsson is perhaps the world's leading authority on understanding expertise and expert performance. His research is the basis for the "ten-year rule" and "10,000-hour rule." This suggests that it requires at least ten years or 10,000 hours of deliberate practice to achieve an expert level of performance in any given domain. In the case of musicians, the number is often closer to 25 years to attain an elite, international level.

Note that the real key here is not the *amount* of practice required. The exact number of hours is debatable, but the *type* of practice that is required to attain an expert level of performance is the key. In other words, just practicing any old way doesn't cut it.

What you want to do, regardless of the time invested, is not do mindless practice. Instead, you need to practice deliberately and mindfully.

What is deliberate or mindful practice? Deliberate practice is a systematic and highly structured activity which is, for lack of a better word, *scientific.* Instead of mindless trial and error, it's an active and thoughtful process of experimentation with clear goals and hypotheses.

You'll find that deliberate practice is draining, given the tremendous amount of energy required to keep one's full attention and resources on the task at hand. The key is to keep tabs on the level of concentration you're able to sustain.

Consider these five keys for effective practice:

1. **Duration.** Keep practice sessions limited to a duration that allows you to stay focused. This may be as short as 10 to 20 minutes.
2. **Timing.** Keep track of times during the day when you tend to have the most energy. This may be first thing in the morning or right before lunch. Try to practice during these naturally productive periods, as these are the times at which you'll be able to focus and think most clearly.
3. **Goals.** Try using a practice notebook. Keep track of your practice goals and what you discover during your practice sessions. The key to getting into the *zone* when practicing is to be constantly striving to have clarity of intention.
4. **Practice smarter, not harder.** Sometimes we need to practice more. There are also times, however, when we don't need to practice harder, but need an altogether different strategy or technique.
5. **Problem-solving model**. Use this as a basis in this way: Pick a target and reach for it. Evaluate the gap between the target and the reach. Return to step one.

I'd emphasize that committed time on a regular basis is better than no time or winging it the next time you want to attain a goal in your work

The last issue is knowing how to practice. In sports, we manage repetition: run a play, swing a bat, etc. In music, we play a section or more.

You may ask: "*How do I practice in business?*" I do so many different things, and my work requires so many different skills, how can I possibly practice?

I agree we can't possibly practice everything we do at work. But many key tasks we perform can be practiced. We need to look at the core items we perform that are key to our success and more important, the success of our businesses, and focus on those core items. For example:

1. **Are you in sales?** Do you role play regularly? Have you effectively prepared for that next sales call or are you winging it?

2. **Are you in marketing?** Have you prepared for your next campaign? Have you reviewed the last campaign and studied how to improve it? Have you attended a webinar or read about the latest, best practices in lead generation, or awareness, and thoughtfully applied these to your campaign and its goals? Can you test these before applying them?

3. **Are you a leader or manager in charge of strategy?** Have you set aside the appropriate time to allow you and your team to work "on" the business and not "in" the business? Have you studied other similar businesses or organizations to see how your business could benefit or avoid their errors?

I'm certain you can reduce your key activities for success to 3 to 5 areas that you must master, like a great athlete or musician, and practice these areas in some fashion to reduce the risk associated with them. More important, you can then make them more successful when you are called on to perform.

Still not convinced? Here's a final thought: When you're not practicing, remember that other people in business somewhere are practicing. And when you compete against them, they will win.

Now's the time to get going and practice.

I'm an Advocate for Advocate Marketing

I'm an advocate for advocate marketing, because I know it works, and it may be the most effective tool in your marketing-communications arsenal. That's why this book, *Advocate Marketing: Building a Customer-Centric Engagement Strategy*, by my friend, Barbara Thomas, or B.T. to those of us who know her and have worked closely with her, is so important and timely.

Check it out on Amazon.com: https://www.amazon.com/Advocate-Marketing-Strategies-Satisfaction-elationships/dp/0134496051/ref=sr_1_fkmr0_1?s=books&ie=UTF8&qid=1501705573&sr=1-1-fkmr0&keywords=Advocate+Marketing%3A+Building+a+Customer-Centric+Engagement+Strategy%2C+by+my+friend%2C+Barbara+Thomas%2C.

Also highlighted in a chapter of the book is a company I co-founded, eBillingHub, and its success.

As I read this highly engaging, informative and practical book, I thought not only about my own business experiences as a serial entrepreneur for the last 30 years at more than a dozen companies, but also what I share with my students as their professor.

For more than ten years, I've had the privilege of teaching business-to-business marketing (B2B) at the University of Pittsburgh, Katz School of Business (MBA). Much has changed in terms of B2B marketing, like the trends I see evolving every year as I prepare my course lessons.

For example, changes have occurred in the product-innovation and development process with the advent of lean and agile methods and processes. But perhaps the most significant aspects of what's changed lies in marketing communications.

In just a few short years, the marketplace has revolutionized the entire art and science of marketing communications in the B2B world. And I believe the changes are good news for us.

What hasn't changed, and is still fundamental, are relationships being at the center of what we're creating and building with all our stakeholders. I've always believed, and I teach my students, that it's all about relationships, whether created in person, online, or by phone.

Of course, we want to build relationships with our customers. But if we can turn them into advocates, the strongest form of any relationship, we create value for our customers and distance ourselves from our competitors.

My definition of marketing, and the one I teach in my course, is reducing barriers to transactions. At the core of that definition are relationships. I continue to learn every day that relationships help to reduce barriers to transactions. In our relationships, we build trust made through deposits in what I call the *Trust Bank Account.*

The question is: How do we leverage these relationships into activity on our behalf to help us be more effective in our marketing and sales activities? Through advocacy, we make our customers and other stakeholders advocates for our businesses. As you will learn in B. T.'s book, advocate marketing not only reduces the barriers to transactions, it also eliminates the barriers you face as marketers, and allows you to drive sustainable, business results.

So why don't more companies do it? Either many fail to appreciate the value of advocacy until it's too late, or they simply don't know how to achieve it. My friend, B.T. removes difficulties like these for you in this highly informative, new book of hers. It's a book and a topic whose time has come despite our highly digital world and virtual connections.

I've been fortunate to work with B.T. several times in my career as a co-worker with her and on joint consulting opportunities. She is, and has always been, a top marketing professional. She knows how to get things done to achieve her businesses goals. And in her book, she lays out one of the most critical elements of success to achieve a sustainable, competitive advantage-customer advocacy.

At the heart of this book lies its value proposition for each of us, whether as marketing practitioners, business persons, or interested readers. Simply stated, that is how to guide and manage what others–most likely your customers–say about you. Knowing how to do that is a must-do in the world we live in, where the buyer controls the selling and marketing processes.

How do I know that? Recent studies tell us customers will contact a sales representative after they've independently completed about 57 percent–some say as high as 90 percent–of the purchasing-decision process. Only 10 years ago, that was 15 percent.

What will your customers and other stakeholders say about you, your brand, and your company?

Having advocates and creating, implementing, and executing a successful advocate-marketing plan can give you and your company the edge you need to cut through all the marketing noise that prospects will find on their buying journey, told not by you, but by your customers.

B.T. has been at the forefront of advocate marketing for years. The rest of us are just now catching up to her. As she points out with her Net Advocate Score (NAS) scoring method covered in her book, we don't want just a promoter, but an advocate. She describes an advocate as "a person who publicly supports or recommends a particular cause or policy."

If you have a promoter who wants to be public about support, you can advance. To paraphrase the Gospel of Matthew 5:15, "No one lights a lamp and then puts it under a basket." Instead, a lamp is placed on a stand.

When I think of advocate marketing, I often think of Peter Secor, as I discuss in just one of the dozen case studies contained in *Advocate Marketing*. For me, Peter defines advocate in many ways. He's a great example of what this book defines, discusses, and shows how to accomplish.

Early in her book, B.T. states, "Advocates are a company's best sales reps ... Advocates proactively influence other people's purchase decisions" and "Advocates are willing to put their reputations on the line for their favorite brands, while forgiving the brand an occasional sub-par performance." I couldn't agree more.

Peter Secor was all these things for me at my company, eBillingHub. He was what I used to call a "sneezer," as in sneezing and others catch the cold. If we delivered the goods for him, he would tell others in his network. We did and guess what? He did as well.

With Peter's' help as a reference, in product feedback, in discussions with other peers, as a speaker for us at events, and much more, we enjoyed the success we did in such a short time.

That success was going from a handful of customers to over 132 in less than 2 years. And that was after struggling for several years beforehand. In short, Peter, as an advocate, helped us build our company. That's the power of advocate marketing.

And armed with this book as your guide, you can begin today, right now. You can start changing customers into advocates, reducing or eliminating barriers as you distance your offerings and your company from competitors.

B.T.'s book shows you the way, whether you're a tiny, one-person start-up or a sophisticated, 100-person operation. In short, you'll find much in its pages that's relevant, useful, and thoughtful.

I know that if I had the information in this book available to me and I had followed B.T.'s advice, the outcomes would have been better. I would have had more Peter Secors and a whole lot less friction.

Have a wonderful journey.

Never Underestimate Your Competition

Success is a lousy teacher. It seduces smart
people into thinking they can't lose.
~ Bill Gates

When the recent presidential election season was in full swing in the United States, we could make many observations. Mine was about competition.

The pundits and experts all thought the election would be between two traditional candidates, both with well-known names and brands. And accordingly, the pundits made their predictions.

Based on these predictions, other well-known names early on decided they couldn't compete in raising money, and decided not to participate. As the race settled in, the two favorite candidates committed what an old boss of mine used to refer to as "drinking your own bath water" or believing your own press.

Unfortunately, everyone in the system forgot to ask a critical part of the process–the voter. That was like not asking your customer or your prospect, which can be dangerous. Even fatal.

Companies of all sizes commit the same business crime of ignoring the competition every day, either because their companies are too small, or their technology sucks, or their people aren't good. Business history is littered with the results of this arrogance with examples of David vs. Goliath.

One of my favorites was Digital Equipment Corporation, or DEC. At its peak late in the 1980s, DEC had $14 billion in sales and ranked among the most profitable companies in the United States. With its strong staff of engineers, the company was expected to usher in the age of personal computers, but Ken Olsen, the autocratic and trend-resistant founder, was openly skeptical of the desktop machines.

Olsen said, "The personal computer will fall flat on its face in business." He regarded personal computers as toys used for playing video games. He's also credited with saying, "There is no reason for any individual to have a computer in his home." And now, you have one in mobile form with you every day and perhaps, even one on your wrist.

More specific than a change in the competitive landscape, potent individual competitors create clear differentiations with their value propositions, and articulate specifically what they will provide and the benefits for their customers.

Think search engines. Did you use Google for a search in the last day? Before 1998, you may have used one of the following: OpenText, Magellan, InfoSeek, Lycos, WebCrawler, Excite, HotBot, AskJeeves, AltaVista, etc.

When Google released its search engine in 1998, its search results were significantly better than those of its competitors. Many people attributed Google's success to its breakthrough technology.

But there was another key reason: Google's stubborn refusal to accept the orthodox view of the time that *stickiness* was crucial to a website's success. Turns out that wasn't true. What was true and contrarian was to think it made business sense to get users off a website as quickly as possible. And you could still make money, lots of it doing that.

Competitors should be taken seriously. All of them. Don't dismiss someone or some company, because they are small or have a crazy idea or say, "Oh that'll never work." About the time you say that, your competitor may just be succeeding and beating you by taking your customers.

More important, your competitors may have something you can learn from and use. There's no shame in leveraging someone else's good ideas. You may remember that Apple, being a terrific fast follower, was not the first in the MP3-player market. Remember that analysts offered mixed reaction to the iPod:

- "It's another incentive that can convince people to buy a Mac."
- "I question the company's ability to sell into a tight consumer market right now."

- "Clearly, Apple is following Sony's lead by integrating consumer electronics devices into its marketing strategy, but Apple lacks the richness of Sony's product offering."
- "The iPod has good features, but this is a pretty competitive category. The question is whether people want that robust of a feature set with that high of a price."

You wouldn't have bet on Apple to win when the company released the iPod. The company was also in poor financial shape and was relegated to niche markets with the Mac. But Apple did succeed, in many ways, because unlike the Apple we know today, competitors and analysts counted the company out.

Do yourself a favor and watch a sporting event. American football, especially college football, is my favorite. Why? Because you really never know who will win. There are upsets every week. Are they really upsets?

Teams regularly state that they "didn't prepare correctly" or "were looking ahead in their schedule" to a bigger game, when they lost to a team to whom they shouldn't have lost.

But sometimes David beats Goliath, like when Michigan loses to Appalachian State or Notre Dame falls to Carnegie Tech or Oklahoma loses for the first time in 48 games. Or for my West Virginia friends, Pitt beats WVU, as it did in 2007.

Do yourself a favor. Take all your competitors seriously. Yes, it's difficult. Yes, we would all like to prioritize our focus on something better. But failing to take your competitors seriously isn't just a mistake. Not doing so can kill your business.

How to Eliminate Your Competition

I n the beginning of the book, *The Road Less Travelled*, the author, M. Scott Peck, writes, "Life is difficult." This is one of the greatest truths. What makes it the greatest truth is that once we comprehend this truth, we transcend it. Once we truly know that life is difficult and accept this, then life is no longer difficult. Once we accept that life is difficult, the difficulty no longer matters.

When faced with the question, who's your competition? I would suggest a similar answer. No matter how much intellectual property, uniqueness or protection we have, we have competition. No matter how different we are as a solution, competitors exist. We must accept that we have competition. Once we do, we can transcend it. Once we accept that we have competition, we can deal with it.

Now you may be saying, "Well, of course we do." or "Everyone knows that." You'd be surprised, however, how often I listen to a pitch for a new startup or someone with an idea that he or she wants to turn into a business, and inevitably someone asks, "Who's your competition?" All too often the reply is, "We really don't have any competition." Yep, it's like clockwork. The words just seem to roll off the tongues of entrepreneur wanabees. But we all know, don't we, that we all face competition. It exists everywhere.

And despite this chapter being titled "How to Eliminate Your Competition," the reality is you can't. And with all due respect to methods like Blue Ocean Strategy, for which I, like many others, have a great deal of respect, these approaches are about understanding your competition and differentiating your company, your product or service, not eliminating it.

Look at it this way: When customers look for a solution, what are their choices?

1. Customers can buy from you.
2. They can buy from a direct competitor.
3. They can use a substitute–some other similar offering or process. Or in the case of many "automation-type" solutions, customers can continue to do things manually.
4. Or, my favorite is customers can do nothing. *Apathy is a competitor.*

Once we accept we have competition, we spend a lot of time identifying direct competitors. We dissect how they sell, what features their products have, where we have advantages, how their pricing works, etc.

We often overlook, especially, in early-market offerings, Number 3 and Number 4 above. This is especially true in B2B companies that often choose to use another way to solve the problem or don't do anything at all.

When apathy wins, it's because the pain of making a change–getting the time, resources, and buy-in to do so–is greater than the pain of leaving things as they are. That's why it's essential to understand not only how your solution addresses a problem, but also what it takes to motivate customers to make a change.

What is the value proposition of your solution relative to apathy? What happens in the short and long term if the customer does nothing?

Lastly, I always like to think of competition as good. If you are the only offering in a marketplace, I'd question if there really is a market. You need at least two players to make it a market.

And as we all know, competition does make us stronger. It keeps us on our toes and focused. In many cases, not having a clear direct competitor weakens our focus and resolve.

So how can you eliminate your competition? You can't. And that difficulty, as M. Scott Peck relayed to us about life, is actually good. Accept it.

Identifying Value in B2B: It's All about Finding Pain or Gain

"A problem well stated is a problem half solved"
~ Charles Kettering

I've had the honor of teaching business-to-business marketing at the MBA level for close to ten years. And I've spent my career practicing B2B Marketing. It's been sobering to see the changes that have taken place over close to 30 years.

But one thing hasn't changed: Understanding who your customer is and specifically, understanding a customer's pain and/or gain to achieve the customer's business goals, roles, tasks, etc. As a matter of fact, it's become more important to understand these aspects of marketing.

Pain and gain were embodied for making B2B sales in early process-oriented sales methodologies. I was trained, like thousands of others, in early sales methods such as Xerox/Learning International–now Achieve Global-Professional Selling Skills (PSS)– a method for B2B selling that was designed more than 40 years ago to train Xerox sales reps how to sell complex products against tough competition. And it proved tremendously successful.

PSS established a method that began with probing or asking open-ended questions.

Here's information from the PSS data sheet regarding probing: allows sales reps to explore how and why it's important-to uncover the circumstances driving the customer's need, as well as the need behind the need. Can you say finding "pain"?

Even then, as process oriented selling strategies were emerging from great companies like NCR, IBM and AT&T. The idea of finding a customer's or a prospect's pain was essential, before just showing up with your 35mm slide deck and being ready to present.

This readiness is even more critical today as customers know more about available offerings to solve their challenges without even talking to a sales person.

I found it fascinating that these same ideas were also essential to the Solution Selling method created by Mike Bosworth in his "nine boxes" that he instructed sales reps to use. The Solution Selling method was all about finding pain, so much so that sometimes gain wasn't mentioned at all.

What was important for the nine-box questioning method was to help the prospect–again through open ended questions–to discover the prospect's latent pain and buying vision or to move the prospect's original vision to a "re-engineered buying vision." The questioning starts with "open" through "control" to "confirm," almost like a mini PSS selling process. Check out this website:https://sales-alliance.com/customized-sales-training-programs/advanced-professional-selling-skills/.

It's all about *diagnosing* before you prescribe.

As I've mentioned in previous chapters, the basics here have been used over and over.

What's more amazing is how in the connected selling world, where 57 percent of the selling process is over before a salesperson is contacted, these skills are even more critical than ever. But more interesting is how they have moved to be more prescriptive not only for selling methods, but also for both marketing communications and overall product and service strategy. Let me illustrate.

For marketing communications, it's about communicating the pain or gain a prospect can find by using an offering we have to sell. Marcom used to talk a lot about features and benefits. Then it moved to problems and solutions.

And with the arrival of positioning, we understood that it was about *who* your customer is, the problem you solved, and why you were different. Even in basic positioning statements, as created by Al Ries and Jack Trout, the method looked like this:

For [target end user],
Who wants/needs [compelling reason to buy] the [product name] is a [product category] that provides [key benefit],
Unlike [main competitor], and
The [product name] [key differentiation].

So many Marcom pros have used this tool for years to create the foundations of messaging and communicating value. And built into this is the identification of pain and gain in its "compelling reason to buy" and "key benefit" and "key differentiation" identifiers. If these items aren't rooted in a prospect's pain or gain, you don't own a position in the customer's mind.

Moving now to strategy, the "Business Model Canvas" (BMC) has become a critical piece of strategy creation since the invention and proposal by Alexander Osterwalder in 2008. (https://strategyzer.com/canvas/business-model-canvas)

As this model has matured, we now have the Value Proposition Design canvas being proposed by the same team that brought us the BMC. (https://strategyzer.com/canvas/value-proposition-canvas)

What is this tool about? It's a plug in for the BMC, matching not only whom you sell to–Segment, Customer's title, Customer's job, Customer's tasks, etc., and then–hey this is interesting–the pain and the gain. And then you match up what you sell to these pain and gain issues. Imagine that. Just like the process oriented selling proposed years earlier.

That's not a coincidence. Why? Because it's fundamental to the complex selling process and doing business with B2B. It's about relationships in B2B, and from these relationships, you need to create the dialogue about pain and gain.

If you can't create the relationship, and in today's B2B marketing world that's done through digital marketing and mostly inbound marketing activities combined through delivering great and consistent content-whitepapers, webinars, infographics, and the like-then you won't get to the discussion to discuss pain and gain.

And as you can see from the Value Proposition Design canvas, it's not sales doing the heavy lifting *after* the product or service has been created or invented. If you haven't figured that out in the beginning of your product ideation, when you identified your customer and did the product or service fit for them in creating your offering, you've got nothing, literally. You can't shine a turd.

Some final thoughts on pain and gain that I share from Michael Skok, an entrepreneur and venture capitalist. (https://www.forbes.com/sites/michaelskok/2013/06/14/4-steps-to-building-a-compelling-value-proposition/#134e23d14695):

> *"A successful venture delivers an order of magnitude improvement over the status quo. If you can't deliver a 10x gain/pain promise, customers will typically default to "do nothing" rather than bearing the risk of working with you. "*

This is key and goes hand in hand with the pain-and gain-discussion. Many of us match the value of what we sell to the customer and think that's it. And then we wonder why sales isn't selling.

First, we need to admit and understand that we always have competition such as direct, substitutes, etc. But the customer can change the customer's behavior-what he does today manually, or even poorly. Doing nothing, apathy, is always a customer option. This holds true, especially when budgets are tight or limited and other priorities exist. This may be the definition of compelling–at least 10 times the gain and pain promise.

Keep this in mind when creating your pain-and-gain promise. Many products linger in this do- nothing hell, because even though your product or service may solve a problem better, it's not enough.

Remember—*it's about pain and gain.* This includes both the match to your segment and your customer and the level you solve. Get it right and you can move ahead. You can turn the customer's pain into your company's gain.

Messaging Alignment: Match Marketing-Communication Goals With Your Sales Goals and Buyers

W hen Obama was still president, I remember watching the State of the Union address one evening. When he related to having equality of pay between men and women he stated, "C'mon people. It's 2015. It's time," I was thinking instead about a blog I had read earlier in the morning

How did I make this connection? It seemed obvious to me at the time that even in 2015, if we were targeting a particular buyer, the messaging that we used should connect with them. That's why it surprised me as I read the blog I'm talking about that it was incredibly technical.

Not that there's anything wrong with being technical It's just that I had been told a month earlier by this same company that they wanted to call on C-level executives and sell their products to them at close to a $200,000 pricing level.

So, I got it. We need to call on multiple individuals in any complex, selling situation. We have what Bill Aulet author of *Disciplined Entrepreneurship* calls the Decision Making Unit, or DMU, which contains everyone from the end user to the primary buyer, to the champions, as well as other influencers, people with veto power, and the purchasing department.

And if you've been selling in a B2B environment, you know there are multiple individuals involved in most decisions. And if you're a student of selling methodologies like Solution Selling or Miller-Heiman, etc., you know the importance of orienting your message to a specific buyer.

When I see one blog as one example of one marketing deliverable, specifically to technical folks, maybe I shouldn't overreact to one blog. So, I looked at the overall messaging of the materials and the site.

As I did, I was wont to put marketing elements into three, simple buckets:

- Awareness,
- Lead generation, and
- Sales support.

Items tend to fit in these three buckets, and this gives everyone, even the financial folks who have to account for these items, a sense of "what is what" and "what it's for."

And voila! As I took a look at the content it was clearly messaged. And the vehicles for the messaging were clearly aimed at one buyer, namely the technical buyer/influencer. But what about the C-level person they wanted to have a meeting with and whom they wanted to close in one 45-minute call (wishful thinking, not reality) –no ROI, no business-value proposition, no nothing for them.

As they would have said at NASA, "Houston, we have a problem."

Great marketing–even good marketing–realizes that the benefit of your product needs to be aligned with various buyer roles, and this is key to help salespeople–they need this messaging to keep the momentum of the sales process moving forward.

An example I often think about in my past is eBillingHub, a SaaS product introduced in 2004, that's owned today by Thomson Reuters and is an incredibly successful offering. But it wasn't always this way.

When I started with the company as its second employee, we had one customer: billing managers. That makes sense you would think. You're selling an electronic-billing solution, and these folks are responsible for ebilling. They understand the problem, and that's whom you should call on. They will understand it and buy it. Right?

Wrong. Again,

Turns out that the billing people/managers were end users and influencers. The real buyer was the VP of Finance or CFO. If the billing manager wouldn't get us to the CFO, they were just "see mores." They'd sit through numerous demos, say nice things, and never buy anything.

We needed to modify the product so it appealed more to the CFO, and we had to modify our marketing materials in all three buckets— awareness, lead gen and sales support, so we could target our messages to them. Without that, we'd have never enjoyed success.

Oh, and one more thing. We learned that the internal, information-technology staff could say "no" to the sale, but not "yes." So, we needed to make sure we had messaging for them as well. All three roles played a part in a successful sale. If we just messaged to the billing manager, no sales took place.

It's nice to want large sales in shorter cycles. It would be great if B2B buyers were more like B2C buyers in that they chose a $100K or $1M product in less than 5 seconds because of brand loyalty or awareness, and that there was only one buyer involved. That's not reality. That's hope.

More important, you need to connect the right messaging to the appropriate buyer. As President Obama said, "C'mon people."

Why Your PR sucks

Do you complain that neither you nor your company gets the media coverage you deserve? Or that when you are included, it's not accurate? Does it really piss you off that you're not getting your fair share of media coverage or the recognition you have worked so hard for? And if only these press people or industry analysts or bloggers or whoever would just do their job, they'd write about you and cover you correctly?

Newsflash: You suck. Maybe not overall. But clearly at PR. Just like a good addiction-recovery program, step one is admission, step two is surrendering and step three is acceptance. Accept that you are responsible for your PR.

Consider this from Alcoholics Anonymous:

"Many have and will fail, usually men and women who are constitutionally incapable of being honest with themselves. They are such unfortunates. They are not at fault; they seem to have been born that way. They are naturally incapable of grasping and developing a manner of living which demands rigorous honesty. Their chances are less than average."

And guess what? Many will fail at PR. Why? Because they blame everyone but themselves. They would rather cry than take action. They would rather complain than do something, like make an investment or give someone ownership in an actual process that pays dividends and creates results.

First, remember that public relations is about what reporters want to write. Advertising is about your paying for it and is about what you want to write or say. So, the burden, rightly or wrongly, is on you to influence reporters and editors at publications to cover things.

Second, are you perfect at your job? Probably not. And like every business that's doing more with less, when you relate to reporters, you're dealing with people who are very busy. They have many subjects and articles to write. The editorial staffs at any publication or news program are smaller than ever before. So, inaccurate articles or unbalanced coverage happens.

Get over it. It's not just you or your company's issue. Everybody complains about press coverage, from the President of the United States to the local Rotary Club. Even the people you think get good press complain they don't get good press or enough of it. And, by the way, that's something to keep in mind as you read any article on any subject.

Third, it's all about relationships. Do you have a relationship with the community of influencers and writers from whom you want valued coverage? If you think these writers are sitting there waiting for your article, your news release, or whatever, you are living under a rock. The year 1955 has left us. Fax machines are no longer in use. It's always best to reach out to a reporter, industry analyst, or whomever the influencer is (social media, blogger, et al) and build a relationship. Awareness and a trust relationship always make for better and more accurate coverage. Period.

And here's something to remember when you don't like an article involving your business or you feel it's inaccurate: Never, ever call or email a reporter and tell him or her that it's wrong and go into detail about where it's wrong. That's a guarantee to be ignored in the future or to have something written about you or your company that you really don't like.

Instead, call the reporter, thank the reporter for the article, even if you don't like it, and mention in a nice way about other parts of the article where you are involved or perhaps the reporter "missed," and offer to help with future articles. That's the way to handle this kind of situation. You can also offer assistance to help with other articles that have nothing to do with you or your desire to get press coverage.

Working in this way helps a reporter to do his or her job and builds a working relationship.

And don't forget that public relations is a profession. If you treat it as less than that, you'll continue to belly ache.

Should Pitch Competitions Die?

Who benefits when money is given away, and is it effective? Pitch contests are still a popular format for entrepreneurs to test their pitching skills and to get awareness of their company, team and business idea. And pitch contests are everywhere.

From a Google search, you can find somewhere between 50 to 100 significant ones happening each year. There are many more, mostly on college campuses, and usually starting in January. Major schools such as the University of Southern California, for instance, have ten different pitch competitions a year.

Pitch competitions are held around the world. Their sole purpose is to give teams of dedicated people an opportunity to pitch their ideas to potential investors, industry advocates, possible partners, and even peers.

If you add up just the different major university pitch contests, millions of dollars and services are given away to help entrepreneurs get their ideas off the ground. Each contest has its rules for eligibility, the panel of judges, and the whole competition venue.

What's the history of these events? The University of Texas started business-plan competitions, with the first Moot Corp in 1984. Moot Corp became Venture Labs Competition three years ago. It's the oldest and possibly most prestigious pitch contest, although Rice University is a serious rival. All of its entrants have won other business plan competitions to get to that one.

Currently, the Rice University contest is the richest. Recent winners have won cash prizes of hundreds of thousands of dollars and total prizes of more than $1 million, including in-kind services like free rent, consulting, legal work, etc.).

Wonderful, isn't it?

Energy. Enthusiasm. Awareness. Networking. What could be better?

How about results? Pitch competitions don't necessarily produce them.

First, let's take a look at the modern pitch contest. Today's pitch contests have "jumped the shark" so to speak. Why?

1. **Money:** Pitch contestants do win money. And it can be substantial. Why they win, however, can have no correlation or meaning for reality. A couple of things on this point:
    - Real-life pitch contests rarely lead to actual investments. Yes, that's true. And unfortunate. The awareness is good, but not meaningful, as it turns out.
    - Keep in mind that no real money is at stake by the judges. The judges, unlike investors, don't have skin in the game. Only the sponsors and donors have an interest, and theirs is a different kind of interest.
2. **Feedback:** Pitch contests are supposed to offer critical feedback for the individuals who pitch, so they can learn and improve. It's educational, but in many cases, they don't get it. Judges in many cases try to stay positive, unlike the Shark Tank TV show. And in some situations, they don't have the opportunity to give verbal or written feedback or both to participants.

    I know in every pitch contest I have run, feedback is the Number-1 request of the participants, especially those who didn't do well or who didn't meet their own expectations. Yet, in many cases, there's no way for them to receive meaningful feedback.
3. **Money Part 2**: As mentioned above, pitchers can get money. Companies can literally live off that money. Yes, some early-stage ideas and teams live off the money while they progress their ideas. Some just live off the money. Yes, that's true.

With little strings tied to the result of the awards, some professional pitchers take advantage of the system, and use the money not to progress the business, but to pay down their own bills or buy something nice for themselves.

What are pitch contests good at?

Entertainment.

First, much of what a startup does is wonky and boring if you don't add some creative pizzazz.

Second, pitch contests are a way to measure how good a communicator you are. They are a great exercise to figure out how to tell your story.

Third, there is nothing like a recital. Being forced to prepare a pitch in a competitive environment gets participants thinking hard about how to message what they are doing.

What to do?

Modern pitch competitions have added all kinds of new elements to shape up participants, teaching them the latest thinking in creating a start-up, such as Lean Launchpad, techniques, and a business-model canvas. This is a good move. Why? Because while creating, practicing and perfecting your pitch is the whole idea of a pitch contest, it's important, especially in a University environment, to balance this with foundational elements such as: "What is the problem?" "What is your value proposition?" And most important, "Who is your customer?"

This is a good start. But it does take away from the focus of a pitch contest and adds more of the elements of an accelerator program. An accelerator program may be more rigorous and need more commitment than participants want or need. And a balance needs to be achieved. And the maturity of participants needs to be understood.

A next step is to hold winners accountable for the money. Participants should tell judges what they are going to do with the money, if they win. They should report what they did with the winnings, even if it was taking a trip or paying off a credit card.

But here is the heart of the issue: Pitching is an important skill. And getting teams to create or improve this skill is important, but should not be the basis of judgment solely for a winning idea.

Keep in mind, no customer buys a product or service because the founder won an award. Customers pay for what solves their problems and improves their lives.

Awards evaluate students on things besides delivering value. They drive and award results that although important, aren't essential. What is essential is for a team to define the problem they are solving, and identify and interview potential customers first. With this comes building a minimum viable product (MVP), and defining, from the feedback and the tests of the MVP, what is the differentiating value proposition. These should be done first.

So, should pitch competitions die? No. But they should change. We have changed so much else about the startup process, why not this?

THE THREE-MINUTE RULE

"The biggest lesson to be learned from this study is that the way (we) begin a discussion about a problem–how you present an issue and how (the other person) responds to you–is absolutely critical." Dr. John Gottman

Recently, I was told about a study by Dr. Gottman who studies relationships. Malcolm Gladwell devoted most of a chapter to him in his huge best seller *Blink*. In a 2007 survey asking psychotherapists to elect the 10 most influential members of their profession over the last quarter century, Gottman was only one of four who made the cut who wasn't deceased.

Dr. Gottman performed a six-year, longitudinal study with fellow University of Washington researcher Sybil Carrère, *Predicting Divorce among Newlyweds from the First Three Minutes of a Marital Conflict Discussion* (1999). This study tested the hypothesis that the way in which a discussion of a marital conflict begins–in its first three minutes–is a predictor of divorce.

This can also be applied to the workplace. According to Christina Tangora Schlachter, author of *Critical Conversations for Dummies,* critical conversation skills can help you address a myriad of problems, including conflict. Like any good, critical conversation, one that's designed to help resolve conflict should follow a common process: examine the issue, options, and ideas; decide on solutions; and then get moving and evaluate the results of the conversation.

This defines a good process that's fine and good with reasonable people willing to cooperate. But what do you do if someone lobs a personal attack at you?

Depending on your temperament, your natural human tendency is to fight, flee or freeze, counter attack, or withdraw. Unfortunately, none of these strategies helps you make progress on your goals in the immediate situation, nor do they put you in a strong position in the long-term.

It's difficult not to take personal attacks personally. It's especially hard when it pushes a button in an already sensitive area, or reminds you of old humiliations from childhood.

Maybe it'll help you to know that personal attacks are rarely about you, the target of the attack. They are about the attacker. Some people, as sometimes seen in public-policy disputes or business negotiations, use intimidation tactics to win a point. For others, you happen to symbolize someone or something they're already unhappy about.

Some individuals thrive on drama and chaos. They create it wherever they go. Some just don't know any better. They may not have learned ways to handle their feelings and frustrations. They may be in the grip of drugs, alcohol, or their own unresolved childhood traumas.

Whatever the reason for the attack, you don't deserve to be treated that way. Although you can't change the other person, you can change the dynamic of the immediate situation in which the attack occurs.

What should you do about workplace conflict? The worst thing you can do is ignore it and pretend it will go away. According to Mitchell Holt, conflict in the workplace often results from a lack of communication. If not confronted, this lack of communication could cause major problems for a business, according to Workplace Issues, a business conflict-resolution resource.

Many businesspeople confuse disagreements with conflicts, but disagreements are differences in opinion that could, but don't always, turn into conflict. Handling disagreements and other forms of possible conflict quickly could change the face of your company. But ignoring them might bring the business down in several ways:

- Decreased Productivity,
- Employee Turnover,

- Divided Teams,
- Poorly Reflected Management, and
- Unhealthy Confrontation.

Bottled-up feelings and unresolved conflict often result in blow-ups, whether that takes the shape of a negative, verbal argument or a physical confrontation.

And this brings us back to the first three minutes. What should you do if you're attacked in the first three minutes of a meeting? According to experts at People Management, you have four options:

- **Walk away.** If a conversation starts to get out of hand, tell the other person that you won't be spoken to in such a way. Say you're willing to talk later, when things are calmer. When you revisit the issue, find somewhere private to have a conversation.
- **Step back.** When someone is attacking you, try to step back from the situation and recognize the action isn't about you. Something else has triggered the emotion in the other person. You just happen to be the unlucky recipient of that emotion. Keep in mind that personal concerns–a sick family member or financial difficulties–can often be behind a co-worker's verbal explosions at work.
- **Remember to breathe.** A natural reaction to a verbal assault is to tense up and begin breathing rapidly or not at all. Become aware of your breathing, taking air in by your mouth and expelling it through your nose. That will help you control your reactions and not behave unprofessionally, even when the other person is acting like a jerk.
- **Set boundaries.** If a co-worker makes a snarky comment about your private life, for example, don't hesitate to tell the colleague that such comments are inappropriate. Make sure you don't try to tell the other person what to do, such as, "You shouldn't talk to me that way." The other person can and probably will, choose to ignore you. Simply focus on what you want by saying, "I don't like it and I want you to stop." Or "I'm not going to listen to this anymore. When you're ready to discuss this professionally, I will talk with you."

Jeanne Brett, the DeWitt W. Buchanan, Jr. Distinguished Professor of Dispute Resolution and Organizations at the Kellogg School of Management, Northwestern University in the *Harvard Business Review*, stated this on the same subject:

"If you decide to let go of a conflict, what do you do instead? Do whatever you can to leave the situation, or at least postpone the conversation. You might say something like: I'm not ready to have this conversation right now. I'm going to step outside to clear my head, and then perhaps, we can meet tomorrow to talk about this."

Those first three minutes can tell us a lot about the future of the relationship, but clearly, we also need to know that we can, and should, walk away when verbally attacked. There's a limit to the abuse you can, and should, take from a colleague. Walking away when conflict spirals limits abuse. It also redirects the conversation from emotions to interests–what's causing the emotions–and opens the door to resolving the problem.

Is Your Company Logo Like "Shimmer"? Two Logos and One Brand?

In a classic, Saturday Night Live parody commercial, Gilda Radner and Dan Aykroyd play a couple having an argument over whether New Shimmer is a floor wax or a dessert topping. Chevy Chase, as a product pitchman, shows them that "New Shimmer is a floor wax *and* a dessert topping!" (http://www.nbc.com/saturday-night-live/video/shimmer-floor-wax/n8625?snl=1)

Shimmer, and why people laugh at this fake commercial, is one of the reasons I'm writing this post. Can one thing do two? Can we understand that in our minds? Do we have time to? Do we have "space" in our brains for this? Specifically, for this post, can two logos represent one organization?

Let's look at the literature. At least my favorite on the subject. In the classic marketing book, *The 22 Immutable Laws of Marketing* by Ries and Trout, several of the Immutable Laws (Notice they don't use the more currently political correct word, "guidelines.") are the following:

- **Law of Exclusivity:** Two companies cannot own the same word in the prospect's mind.
- **Law of Focus**: The most powerful concept in marketing is owning a word in the prospect's mind.
- **Law of Sacrifice**: You have to give up one thing to get another.
- **Law of Resources**: Marketing is a game fought in the mind of the prospect. You need money to get there, and you need money to stay there as well. Without adequate funding, an idea won't get off the ground.

These are four really important laws for this post. Why?

My alma mater, after just changing its logo back to its traditional logo from the late 1970's for a "retro" look, now has selected a second logo for the same organization. In short, it now has two logos for one organization. In its defense, they would tell you it introduced a second logo for the academic's portion of the organization, keeping the retro one for athletics only. They see them as two different things evidently. And they are not the only University. Look at UCLA. Clearly, they agree. (http://brand.ucla.edu/brand/print/logo/)

Hmmmmm.

Again, maybe it's me. I watch in awe the GEICO commercials. GEICO uses the Gecko, and also use several others (think caveman ads). No other brand in the history of advertising has used so many branded characters and ads with differing tones and messages at the same time. The rationale? The goal of multiple campaigns is to be noticed in a hyper-competitive category with an essentially difficult-to-differentiate commodity. OK, I can buy that even though I disagree. But hey, it works for them. So, what do I know?

Here's my issue: A logo mark is an actual image that identifies a company and may or may not include the company's name. Put another way, your logo is a graphic communications vehicle of your brand. Why would you want your customers to think of two things?

Remember: You're not a monopoly. You may think you're the center of the universe and the distinction in your two separate parts of your business is important. But you do have competition! It's called trying to create a space in your prospect's mind, and that space needs to represent the unique value you have. And you think that's easy?

There's the old urban myth from J. Walker Smith that says we've gone from being exposed to about 500 ads a day back in the 1970's to as many as 5,000 a day today. Even if that's inaccurate, advertising clutter is the single, biggest problem with marketing. Not just today, but as long as advertising has been around. People are annoyed by ads that show up in unfamiliar places, but become used to them over time. So, marketers respond by finding even more unfamiliar places. It's cumulative and it's getting worse. Yet, consumers can process no more information today than they could before, and perhaps even less. Multi-tasking is just a fancy word for paying little attention to many more things at once. If we really want to do good marketing, then we have to get out of the clutter business and stay solidly in the communications business.

Logos are a lot like fingerprints. Each one is a distinctive mark that tells the world who you are. The goal is to create a logo that represents your brand in look and feel and becomes synonymous with your business.

Your customers don't care about you; they care about themselves and how you solve their problems. And multiple logos confuse your customers, give off mixed signals, and dilute your marketing and branding efforts. And this is costlier to maintain.

The bottom line is this: Don't be difficult to do business with. Reduce the barriers to any transaction, including how potential customers recognize who you are. One brand and therefore one logo can't stand for two different things. Choose.

SMALL IDEAS DON'T MAKE STARTUPS SUCCEED. BIG IDEAS DO

When I began my career in startups, back in 1985 (32 years ago) at a little remembered startup company here in Pittsburgh called American Robot that later became Cimflex Teknowledge, events like this didn't exist in Pittsburgh. Since then, the region has grown economically stronger through the cooperation of entrepreneurs, universities and economic-development organizations.

Over time, I've reflected on what makes companies, start-up or otherwise, succeed and I've concluded that good ideas don't build success, big ideas do. Consider what big ideas do:

We have a therapy that could reverse Type 1 diabetes. We have break throughs for the targeted delivery of drugs and single-use sunscreen pills for getting sunscreen right. As a person who gets tan the way I do, I need this pill when summer rolls around.

These are big ideas. And to see these big ideas come to reality takes more than hard work, strong investments and a dose of good luck. Why? Because start-ups combine big ideas while entrepreneurs work under extreme uncertainty. This combination defines what a startup is: an organization dedicated to creating something new under extreme uncertainty. And I can tell you that working at the intersection of big ideas and extreme uncertainty can be the ride of your life.

Every day in my calendar, I get those "Today in History" messages. Do you get these? Recently, I noticed that the Bank of England was formed 323 years ago and was headquartered on Threadneedle Street in London. This location has special meaning for me that I shall explain later.

Moving up a bit in time, in November 1986, I joined a company, Duquesne Systems, that had about $5 million in sales. I was 26, and joined the company as its first product manager.

Duquesne Systems was founded on the big idea that software could manage and operate other software.

I remember a meeting we had after I joined the company, when one of founders announced that we were going to hit $100 million by 1990. I thought that was not only a little crazy, but as someone responsible for revenue, maybe even a little unreasonable.

But it was a big idea, or what Jim Collins in his seminal book, *Built to Last* refers to as a BHAG, A big, hairy, audacious goal. And let me tell you, from where we were at the time, there was a lot of big uncertainty.

Let me put a little bit of my world at that time in perspective. Just five years earlier, I had graduated with a degree in engineering at the University of Pittsburgh, had worked as a sales person at EATON Corp Cutler-Hammer, a company then headquartered in Milwaukee and now, located in Pittsburgh.

I had just finished my MBA going to night school, a program that had rejected me three times before I was admitted. At 26 years of age, I had never been to the West Coast, let alone Europe. And I came from a typical Pittsburgh family. A big vacation in my family when I was growing up was a trip to Erie, Pennsylvania.

But I remember April 4, more specifically April 4, 1990. On that day, and because of a big idea, I was having high tea with the Managing Director of the Bank of England on Threadneedle Street in London at the age of 29, as the Vice President of Marketing and Product Management for LEGENT Corporation.

The reason I remember April 4 is that on this date, Duquesne Systems merged with Morino Associates to become a $100-million company, and one of the world's top-10 software companies. On this day, I experienced that big ideas could become reality.

Since then, I've been involved in many other start-ups, some notable, some not so much, some great successes and some grand failures. But all of them started with a big idea. At AXENT Technologies, where

I led product marketing, we had the crazy idea in 1994 that people would buy software to improve their security on this thing then called the "Information Superhighway." We grew that company with big ideas and with things called "firewalls" to $125 million in sales. We sold the company to Symantec in 2000 before the dot-com crash for $1 billion.

In the last several years, some friends and I had the big idea that we could automate the billing in law firms. We knew this was a big idea, because one of the founders, an attorney, used to say, "'You know, law firms only do two things: lawyering and billing."

We thought we could do one of them—billing—better. This was a big idea. And we started eBillingHub. Besides that, eBillingHub provided its software in a thing called the cloud. This, back in 2006. Can you imagine lawyers billing data being in a cloud? That's a big idea. The company was so big, and it grew so rapidly that in less than three years we sold it to Thomson Reuters, one of the largest names in professional services, and specifically in legal software.

Now, I find myself as an Executive in Residence, a part of the great University of Pittsburgh, helping to commercialize software. And I can tell you that in and of itself, this is a big idea.

The University of Pittsburgh isn't known for software, but I can tell you that software does live here. Software abounds all over the campus in our School of Computing, in the School of Information Sciences, in our Engineering School, in the Katz Business School and many other places.

And while we may not be hailed yet as that "other school" in the Oakland community of Pittsburgh, we have some pretty good software. We're getting there. It may surprise you to know that the University of Pittsburgh has software inventions in all the hot areas of software and IT today. In social media, in cloud computing, in big data and decision support, in mobile apps, and more.

Big ideas like these present great opportunities for entrepreneurs like me and others to build the next set of great companies in the Pittsburgh region.

Henry Ford once said, "I am looking for a lot of men who have the infinite capacity to not know what can't be done." So, I encourage all of you to think bigger and to have grander ideas. Small ideas will get lost in the noise from the rest of the world, but big ideas will be heard because of their sheer audacity.

It's difficult to think big. The world is constantly telling you what can't be done. It's easier to think small, because small moves have less risk, less reward and less visibility. There are millions of small ideas tumbling around in the worldwide entrepreneurial conversation at any time.

But big ideas are crazy and inconceivable. They polarize people and people react to them, strongly and emotionally. Big ideas challenge people. They start talking about a crazy, big idea, and the virus spreads.

Small ideas don't make the world go around. Big ideas do. If you're going to be an entrepreneur and take the risk, then commit yourself to the grand adventure of a big idea.

PROMOTING MULTIPLE PRODUCTS WITHOUT CONFUSING YOUR TARGET AUDIENCE

Dealing with multiple offerings, the channel and one market? If you've ever worked for a growing company that was adding new products (offerings) or acquiring new products for your salesforce to sell, you may have run into the issues of the go-to-market plans for each product. Especially as a young product manager, even in one of my earliest companies back in the 1980's, we experienced this concern, in messaging to the sales organization and the customer.

As I've participated in many companies and consulted with hundreds more, I've seen the issue come up often: How do we capture the mind share of the channel–or channels–and our customers, not confuse them, and maximize our opportunities.

At first, it looks daunting. How can we organize our promotional activities so that we can achieve this goal? How do we align them with the strategy of our company and the revenue goals or other goals of our organization?

It seems like you should jump in and give each product (offering) its time or space.

Don't. Mistake. Bigly.

First, every product manager, department or division would love to have the channel to itself, even for a small period of time. But if you're leading the organization, you need to promote the whole message of what you offer, not just a portion of it.

You need to stay focused on messaging the overall goals of the company, regardless of the product(s). And another important thing: You're not the customer. What you choose to promote while other offerings are not being promoted may not be what customers want to purchase. Are you smart enough to decide that? Ah no. Because you're not really the decision maker. First, let your sales team be the problem solver. Let your salespeople use the products in their bag to bring value to the customer as they need it, when they need it. Your job is to promote your overall organization and its value proposition. That's the first step to eliminating having to decide which product to promote and when.

Second, your customer is not one, monolithic market. You know that. If you don't, then go back to Marketing 101 and read about customer segmentation. Your customers don't have just you to purchase from, and even the narrowest market has various segments. Your offerings will appeal to them because of their natural differences, unless they are the same. While you are promoting your product A, your product B is getting its teeth kicked in by competitive product B offerings.

Third, yes, you will have times when you promote one product more heavily for some reason like timing or discount, etc. But that doesn't mean you can't promote another. The customer interested in the new car and the one who wants an oil change may be on your same target list, and be in the same customer base, but they are different.

Here are some basic market-segmentation definitions to consider:

- **Identifiable**: Can your company identify and measure the differentiating attributes of the segments?
- **Accessible**: Are the segments reachable through various communication and distribution channels?
- **Substantial**: Are the segment sizes large enough to justify needed resources?
- **Specialized needs**: Are there valid justifications for having multiple segments? Does each segment address different needs?
- **Durable**: Are the segments stable, so that there is minimal, restricting impact with each change to existing products or the introduction of new products?

Get this right for your one-customer audience, and then, target the appropriate offerings. You'll find that doing promotions at the same time doesn't confuse anyone. Your customers are smarter than you think. And the only one who is confused is you or some selfish product managers who want the marketing machine to themselves.

Take the time to understand your customers and to target their needs. Understand your market and the customer segments your offerings appeal to. It works.

SECTION 1 QUIZ

Test Your Knowledge from Section 1

1. What are the elements of integrated marketing communications?
2. How does author and marketing expert, Eric Ries, define a startup? What does this definition suggest that entrepreneurs do when launching a startup?
3. According to Al Ries, there are 22, immutable laws of marketing. Can you name four of them?
4. Public relations is all about building relationships. Building relationships with whom?
5. Of the five ways you can practice in business, name three.
6. What are the three, fundamental questions to ask when creating a business strategy?
7. What do customers really want to buy? Products/services that are better or that are different?
8. Are product-line extensions good or bad in marketing your product(s)?
9. What are the four questions you need to ask when you develop a strategy for your business?
10. When marketing, you have to think about positioning your product or service to prospects. How do you define positioning?

Answers to Section 1 Quiz

1. Integrated marketing communications is the application of consistent brand messaging across traditional and non-traditional marketing channels and using a variety of promotional methods that reinforce each other. (**Choose Wisely. Just Because You Can Pick Up a Pencil Doesn't Mean You Can Write**)

2. A startup is an "organization dedicated to creating something new under conditions of extreme uncertainty." This definition suggests that entrepreneurs address the issues of why they need to test and iterate to reduce risk and to get better outcomes. (**Starting a Startup: The Science of Creating a New Business**)

3. **Law of Resources**: Marketing is a game fought in the mind of the prospect. You need money to get there, and you need money to stay there. (**Source: Is Your Company Logo Like 'Shimmer'? Two Logos and One Brand**)

4. It's always best to reach out to a reporter or industry analyst, or whomever the influencer is–social media expert, blogger, et al–and build a relationship. Awareness and a trust relationship always make for better and more accurate coverage. (**Why Your PR Sucks**)

5. When it comes to business, practice can involve studying best practices, seeking guidance from mentors and coaches, practicing a difficult conversation with a trusted advisor, attending a webinar, or reading an eBook about key subjects in your profession or that affect your job. These are all ways to practice and prepare in business. (**Three Reasons Why You Need to Practice in Business**)

6. Who is the target customer? What is the value proposition for that customer? What are the essential capabilities needed to deliver that value proposition? (**Your Business Strategy: By Design or Default?**)

7. Customers buy different, not better. They remember different, not better. Think about yourself, your products and services, and your company, and ask, "Why are we different?" By being

different, you may surprise yourself how much better you really are. (**Different Beats Better**)

8. But, for all the perceived benefits, the costs of line extensions are dangerously high. That's because the strategic role of each product becomes muddled when a line is over segmented. A company that extends its line risks undermining brand loyalty. (**The One Thing You Need to Remember About Product-Line Extensions**)

9. How attractive is the market? Where will we compete? How will we compete? What is the financial impact? (**Strategy: The Four Questions**)

10. Positioning is how you differentiate yourself in the mind of the prospect. (**How to Stand Out in a Noisy Market: Defeating the "Me To"**)

Section 2: How to Put Your Sales Hat On

I have This Idea for a New Product And I Wanted to Know, "What Do You Think About It?"

I get this question a lot in my role as Director of the Blast Furnace at the University of Pittsburgh's Innovation Institute from students, faculty and staff. It's actually amazing just how many times a week I hear this "I have this idea" question from someone looking for my reaction to it. And I wonder whether the person has truly discovered the next *startup unicorn* idea that will turn him or her into the next Steve Jobs.

Let's discuss the issues with this question.

First, and please repeat this: "Forget Your Idea."

Yes, no one cares.

Your new service, your new product, your cool widget, your neat app, your disruptive, next- generation-100 percent "buzzword compliant" invention is not important to me at this point. Here's why:

As a prospect, I have problems in achieving my goals. Can you help me with these problems? If so, I want to talk. If not, I don't care about what you've invented or what you're selling.

What's important, and where to start in a dialogue with prospects or customers, is with the problem(s) you're solving.

Remember this:

- Ideas come from problems.
- Problems come from customers.

In the words of Justin Wilcox, "Customers don't buy products. Customers buy solutions to problems."

Identify the problem, then your customers, and you'll be well on your way to discovering if you have a good business idea. And you don't have to ask me.

But if you still want to ask me what I think about your idea, let's address a second issue. To be as clear as I can, in most cases, I'm not the target audience for many of the ideas that people pitch me.

Greg Coticchia is not your target segment or market. I could be, but chances are I'm not. That said, I appreciate your wanting to share with anyone, including me, your idea. This is much better than the "I can't tell you anything about my idea, because you'll steal it" approach that many entrepreneurs have.

And of course, doing any type of customer discovery should be encouraged. But when you pitch someone, think about *why* you're doing it. Are you asking me what I think of your idea as a business? As a potential investor? As a potential buyer of your solution? What persona are you testing with the question? With this decided, frame the question and the information you share in that context.

But let's go back to the problem issue. It deserves more thought. If potential customers (prospects) recognize the problem, that's great! That may mean there's a potential problem that customers recognize. If people don't recognize the problem, you could be in the early stage of a market, or in a market that no one cares about. Remember, when you do have a solution, customers can choose to do four things:

1. Buy from you.
2. Buy from a competitor.
3. Buy a substitute, a different way to solve the same problem.
4. Do nothing. In this case, your competitor is apathy.

Now the question goes to market size. There's only one thing worse than no customers and that's one customer. Is there a market, or more important, a particular market segment that wants to pay to solve a problem? There may not be. Or customers may not want to pay a lot.

If you only have a handful of prospects, or they don't want to pay a lot, or both, you may have identified a problem not worth solving. In other words, nice job identifying the problem, but it's not a business.

Let's say you identified a problem. And you know who the potential customer or market segment is; you know a lot of customers exist in that segment with that problem, or enough customers at the price they are willing to pay for you to grow a profitable business.

Only then should you mention your solution. That's when your "I have this idea" comes into play.

The lesson for today is this: Forget the idea and focus on the problem: **What is the problem? Who has it? And how big is the problem?** Start there and evaluate that first. Then the product-market fit will come.

The Secret 8 Steps to Startup, Customer Attraction and Sales

I n 2014, I was asked to guest lecture a class on customer attraction at the prestigious Carnegie Mellon University (CMU) Heinz School. Since I work for the University of Pittsburgh, I refer to CMU as "that small, private school up the street."

Being asked to lecture on this process prompted me to reflect on the specific steps I've used in the past that have driven sales for the many startups, small businesses, and large enterprises I've been involved in over my 30-plus-year career.

I know these steps may not be as revealing or insightful as Eric Ries's *The Lean Startup* or Steve Blank's *The Startup Owner's Manual* for those who want to apply these steps to building a business. But hey, I guarantee it will take less time to read this chapter than their books.

A word of caution: It's easy to list a set of steps, like a recipe, and think that by simply following the directions, the outcome will be successful. As we know with preparing any meal, it doesn't work that way. You need a great chef, the right tools, and a terrific team. Knowing the recipe and ingredients is, however, still helpful. So here they are:

- Define your product or service, your WHAT.
- Identify your ideal customer, your WHO.
- Differentiate yourself from the competition, your WHY.
- Establish a beachhead, your WHERE.
- Define and build your channel, your HOW.

- Develop awareness, your WHEN.
- Satisfy your customer.
- Stay consistent and focused.

This is pretty straightforward, but reality is more difficult. Let's run down each briefly:

1. **Define your product or service**. This is the *what* you're doing. Some key questions you have to ask: What is it that your customers are really buying? For example, you may be selling web-based software tools, but your clients are buying increased productivity, improved efficiency and cost savings. Think benefits! And think about what pain customers and prospects may have or about the gain you're providing for them.

   So, think: What problem does your service solve? What need does your product meet? What want does it fulfill? And get that to a focused list that you can absolutely make sure resonates with your customers.

2. **Identify your ideal customer.** This is the *who* you're selling to and *who* will buy your offering, i.e. your product or service or both. It's key to get as specific and as granular as possible when you select a market segment, defined by identifiable, accessible, and substantial. It's important as well, if you are in B2B sales, that you know specific titles of potential buyers or specific demographics, if you have a B2C offering.

   Remember, the Fortune 500 is not a market segment. That's a list. And a target group is as much about focus as it is about knowing what to rule out. Everything to everyone is nothing to no one. So, choose and be as specific as possible. And then, focus on those buyers and don't say, "Yes" to anyone else.

3. **Differentiate yourself from the competition**. This is *why* you're different and *why* anyone should care about what you have to sell to them. I had a great mentor, Jack Roseman, who used to ask me and other budding business people a critical question that reminds me of this step: Why do you deserve to be in business?

Great question. Ask yourself that and it may help you answer the reason why you're different or better or both than your competition.

And if you think you have no competition, think again. There's always competition–direct competition, indirect competition, substitute competition and my favorite, apathy.

Customers always have choices. Ask yourself *what's* competing for the potential client's money? What is it and why should the potential customer spend his or her money with you instead? If you've answered these questions, you've defined your competitive advantage or unique selling proposition.

4. **Establish a beachhead**. This is your *where,* and this allows you to focus your marketing efforts and to dominate your market. It's essential to build an initial set of lighthouse customers to establish feedback for your offering, from whom to gain feedback, and to start building a repeatable, scalable way to go to market. Getting your first set of customers will also give initial credibility to your offering.

   I like beachhead strategies. The term comes from military strategy, meaning that as you invade enemy territory, you need to focus your strength and concentrate on winning a small area, the beachhead that becomes the stronghold from which you'll advance into the rest of the territory.

   And it's good business. In business, particularly startups, the beachhead strategy is about focusing your resources on one key area, usually a smaller market segment or product category, and winning that market first, even dominating that market, before moving into larger markets.

5. **Define and build your channel**. This is *how* you get your offering to market. You need to decide the critical aspect of how you will go to market. Will it be through direct sales? Indirect sales? Telesales? Telemarketing? Web based? In short, your selection of a distribution channel is critical.

   It's a cost issue. What does it cost for you to obtain a customer, and does your channel selection allow you to do that cost effectively? It's a marketing and messaging issue. Does the channel match the value proposition and pricing of your product? You aren't buying that new Mercedes C Class at Costco. And does it get you to your target customers and allow them to purchase in a familiar and expected way?

There are no simple answers to these questions. To highlight the complexity of channels today, consider Apple. The company sells directly and indirectly. It has its own brick and mortar stores and brick and mortar resellers, sometimes directly adjacent to its stores. Apple sells its own products and makes tremendous revenue and profits from reselling music and apps. Apple has upended the traditional notion of sales channels. Yet, Apple and its partners continue to flourish. Not every company can be the next Apple, but we should all learn from its successes.

6. **Develop awareness.** You need to have a high level of awareness and be able to be found when the customer or prospect wants to find you and your offering. It's simply impossible for potential clients to buy your product or service, if they don't even know or remember it exists.

Generally, a potential customer will have to be exposed to your product 5 to 15 times before he or she is likely to think of your product when the need arises. That's a lot of marketing. And it's estimated by several sources that in recent years, we're exposed to more than 5,000 commercials daily.

The exact number may be hard to agree on, but it becomes exponentially higher with every passing decade. This clutter of ad exposure runs head on into the ever-constant, cognitive capacity of human beings. You may care about your offering and think that everyone knows about it, but they don't. It's a constant battle even for the best marketers and brands.

And needs often arise unexpectedly. You must stay in front of your clients consistently, if they are going to remember your product or service when their needs arise. That's why having content on your web site and being easy to find on the web is so essential. Almost all of us begin our search to fulfil any new need by doing a Google search and seeing what's out there.

In developing awareness, you shouldn't have to waste a lot of resources. But beware. You can easily waste resources as you focus on the awareness that will drive customer acquisition. Another way of saying that is to focus on lead-generation activities like inbound marketing, email, and the like versus general awareness activities like advertising. Some advertising opportunity could amazingly lead to explosive growth, but your odds are probably better buying a lottery ticket.

Building a strong, customer-acquisition engine is the best chance you have of creating long-term awareness. At a certain scale, using advertising to build awareness for brand building makes sense. But a lot of solely awareness activities can be a total waste of money.

7. **Satisfy your customer.** It's not over yet. You work hard to acquire customers. But don't let them go. Customer churn is inevitable, but how much you experience is under your control. Nurturing relationships with your customers is a crucial part of growing a successful business. And in this age of automation and innovation, caring for your customers has never been more important.

   At any moment, an unhappy customer can share his or her opinion with the masses through social media and/or the web and negatively affect your business. That's why it's more important than ever to create an excellent experience for your customers to help develop your company's relationship with them into love.

   Walt Disney said it best, "Do what you do so well that they will want to see it again and bring their friends."

8. **Stay consistent and focused!** Finally, remember what got you there. Stay true to what got you the success you are enjoying. Successful companies stay focused on their customers. And knowing customer needs and wants must be an important part of any company's growth strategy.

   Day-to-day pressures can take a company off track and cause it to lose that all-important customer-centric perspective. If you stray from what you've been doing, make sure you're doing it for the right reason. Don't do it for the one big deal outside of your core capabilities. You'll regret it. There's only one thing worse than no customers. That's one customer, in the wrong market.

Those are my 8 steps to customer attraction. I hope you enjoyed it. Every business wants to get customers, keep them and add to their numbers, but it's never easy. I hope this set of steps helps you on your business journey. Let me know what you think.

SILVER-BULLET SELLING

"In folklore, a bullet cast from silver is often the only weapon that's effective against a werewolf, witch, or other monsters. Sometimes, the silver bullet is inscribed with Christian religious symbolism, such as a cross or the initials, "J.M.J" (Jesus, Mary & Joseph)"

At times, we wish we had a silver bullet for making sales, particularly in B2B selling. If the prospect would just listen to what we have, and understand its value, then we would make more sales. Or so we think.

But B2B sales have long complex selling cycles with multiple people involved. This isn't like buying Cheerios at the grocery store.

I recently heard about a young, startup company that was focusing on getting the right words in its presentation for its sales reps to state so that prospects would immediately understand the problem the company solved and buy more quickly. They had spent months on this and were still working on it.

One venture capitalist I worked with years ago used to call this process "studying your navel."

The reality is this: *The right words don't exist. Stop looking.* You'll never get the PowerPoint just right so that salespeople can just repeat the words verbatim and the purchase order will take place. Ain't happening. There is no silver bullet.

You need to get out what the inventors of the Lean Startup Methodology called "getting out of the building." I call it "getting bloodied."

I was once an advisor to eBillingHub, a firm now owned by Thomsen Reuters. The company simplified the electronic-billing process for lawyers. Management was stuck. They had only four customers and less than $150,000 in revenue after about four years in business. They were ready to shut the doors.

Were they early in the market? Was it a solution no one wanted? Did the company's electronic- billing process provide any value?

Frustrated with where they were as a business, and where they weren't going, they gave me the opportunity to come into the business as a founder and CEO to see if I could drive up sales in the go to market business.

At the time, I had no experience in the legal space and no contacts with law firms. I had never worked with electronic billing or even a billing application. In short, I had no domain experience or contacts.

But I did have a beginner's mind. I didn't know what couldn't be done. That was an advantage. I also had years of experience in selling early-stage, enterprise-software solutions. I knew what worked in other spaces. And this was an arsenal of knowledge I could rely on to help the company succeed. And I had two ears and one mouth that I could use equally well with prospects and partners.

So, there we were, two people. The other folks were part time or had full-time jobs. We worked out of a second bedroom of a townhouse in a remote suburb of Pittsburgh, one selling and marketing, the other coding and servicing. That was our company. Nothing else. Oh, and very little cash. And no pipeline. So, we got bloodied.

We figured out that billing managers in big law firms were the logical persons to call on; unfortunately, billing managers were only the influencers and not the decision makers.

We also figured out that the IT person could say, "No" and not "Yes," and in many cases, this was not a good way into an account. Because IT people didn't have any pain. They didn't do the billing and didn't care. They also thought they could build the solution themselves.

Finally, we realized that we needed to call high, the Chief Financial Officer (CFO). But being an unknown company with an early-stage product made this difficult. We needed to get to billing manager leaders so they would take us to the chief financial executives.

How did we learn all this? By making lots of mistakes. By asking stupid questions. By bumping into walls. And every once in a while, by pissing off prospects.

It turned out that we had to modify the product to appeal more to CFOs. We had to demo the product differently, using more of role based approach than a features approach. And we needed to learn that the largest law firms were not the segment to build a business with initially, because they didn't have the problem we were fixing at that time.

We learned a lot by getting bloodied.

We found all this out, not by tweaking the positioning or the messaging, or revising the Power Point deck for the umpteenth time. No, we found it out by preparing, practicing, learning, and listening. We carefully learned our patterns of what was working and what was not when we interacted with prospects.

And never, ever did we think we knew it all or were arrogant because of our past success. We knew we would make all new mistakes and if we didn't move quickly, we wouldn't have a business.

The result: We went from 4 customers to 32 in 9 months. And the next year, we ended with 105 customers, and yes, that did include some of the world's largest law firms in the AmLaw 200, the Fortune 500 of law firms list. The company had a great exit with multiple large, time-and-billing firms wanting to purchase it. It was a great ride.

So, quit looking for the silver bullet. It doesn't exist. And get out of the building and get bloodied. The knocks will be tough, but you'll push through.

Bad news early is good news. Find out what you have now and what you don't and you will be that much ahead tomorrow. And stop hunting for the silver bullet.

B2B Selling: Stop Showing Up and Throwing Up

I recently heard about a CEO of a stalled startup trying to regain growth, who instructed his sales reps to get appointments with C-level prospects and do a 45-minute presentation about his company and its offerings.

When one of the reps said that in his years of experience, he had never sold that way, he was told, "Well, that's how we do it here."

I found that reply amazing. And even more so that it was said in 2017.

It's been nearly 40 years since Neil Rackham invented SPIN Selling. If you aren't familiar with Mr. Rackham and his work, here's a recap. While he was a post-graduate research fellow at Sheffield University, Rackham developed new, research tools to study areas like selling and negotiating where success depended on complex, inter-personal skills.

He created a research consortium, supported by major multinational companies, including Xerox and IBM, and raised the funds needed to complete a research study of successful selling. This project involved a team of 30 researchers who studied 35,000 sales calls in more than 20 countries. Rackham published the results of these studies in his books *SPIN Selling* and *Major Account Sales Strategy*.

SPIN ushered in the modern era of B2B selling. SPIN stands for four types of questions related to selling–Situation, Problem, Implication, and Need Payoff. These questions come into play during the lengthy investigation phase of any sales meeting.

What Rackham researched, discovered, and codified is what successful B2B reps do. They ask prospects questions to expose their pain and then save them with their products or services.

Here, I spend time with SPIN and Neil Rackham because I consider, rightly or wrongly, that his work has fundamentally changed B2B sales, and his approach is embedded into many of the other sales systems in use today. Here's an overview of SPIN:

"*SPIN*" stands for the four question types asked in sequence that are needed to land a sale.

S stands for Situation Questions. Data-gathering questions about background and facts about the company you're calling on.

P stands for Problem Questions. Questions that explore problems, difficulties, and dissatisfactions in areas where your product or service can help.

I stands for Implication Questions. These types of questions take a client's problem and explore its effects or consequences.

N stands for Need Payoff Questions. These types of questions get the client to tell you, the salesperson, the benefits that your solution could offer.

Sales reps who took the time to follow the SPIN steps won more business. They understood the situations prospects were in and defined clearly the problem prospects had. And this is key: they understood the implications (impacts) of problems, made progress with deals and then explained how specific benefits, not features, of their products or services could resolve issues. Rackham's genius is that he studied why some B2B sales people were more effective at sales than others. Those who didn't "show up and throw up," who actually asked questions and listened to prospects, who truly understood the pains or gains of specific business problems, were more effective and sold more. Period.

In the mid to late 70s and throughout the 80s, large companies like Xerox, IBM, AT&T and others trained the best reps. Other companies liked hiring these reps, because they were so well trained.

And business schools didn't teach sales. And many still don't today, which is a sad, even tragic commentary, given the importance of sales to any leader or manager.

As I wrote earlier, there are only two problems in business–not enough sales and everything else. Learning about B2B sales is essential to success.

Xerox, and later its spinoff, Learning International, turned much of Rackham's work into Professional Selling Skills (PSS). For those of us who remember that, I still have the question card in my wallet. Even in those days, we learned the value of open-ended questions to discover pain and then confirm it with closed ended questions. That was basic stuff even 30-plus years ago. Today, SPIN is owned and taught by the Huthwaite Group.

Some Classic B2B Sales Methods

As a result of Rackham, and the general ineffectiveness of showing up and throwing up, many others created new B2B selling methods, all based on similar ideas:

Solution Selling: Frank Watts developed the sales process dubbed "solution selling" in 1975. Then, Mike Bosworth founded Solution Selling in 1983, based on his experiences at Xerox Corporation on a SPIN selling pilot project. Solution Selling is fundamentally based on the idea that customers will only be motivated to buy something if they identify there's a need. And because there are times when prospects are not even aware there's a problem, the questions a salesperson asks are key.

Customer Centric Selling (CCS): Similarly, Customer Centric Selling, also founded by Mike Bosworth, is about finding a prospect's pain. How? By helping customers uncover their needs through probing questions. Not by getting an appointment and then doing death by PowerPoint for 45 minutes. CCS is based on the premise that if you can elicit what a customer actually needs, instead of just a stated want, you can better serve a customer and tailor your selling and offering accordingly.

Sandler Sales Method (SSM): Sandler has been a successful method for many years. The Sandler methodology reflects a conversational sales mode, with a "pull" process instead of a "push" process. Sandler also recognized that most salespeople throw a great deal of product knowledge at potential customers. Like the others above, the Sandler sales methodology focuses on pulling people in, and using knowledge of the product throughout the buying process.

The Sandler Methodology also gives salespeople the ability to take "no" from a prospect when and if there is no clear, client desire to proceed or ROI. If the numbers don't add up, then it's okay to accept that there's no fit.

As Sandler sales people describe it themselves, the key differences of Sandler selling come down to the qualification process of asking questions. Many other good sales methods exist, but I'm not going into detail about them here, like Miller-Heiman, Complex Sales, Challenger Sale, etc. Nonetheless, the pattern is clear. None of what these sales methods prescribe is new.

Any modern sales method (in the last 40 years) is about understanding the prospect, the situation, the needs, identifying a prospect's pain and gain, and then aligning a solution to move the deal forward. All of which means that great sales people don't talk much. They listen and ask good questions.

The conclusion is that if you're still telling your sales reps to go forth and do a 45-minute presentation to a high-level executive, you're going to lose. You don't understand the length and complexity of B2B sales. And you are already 40 years behind. You simply don't understand what sales is about or how to lead and manage it.

Prospects Complete 57 Percent of the Sales Cycle

What's worse for sales people now is that the Internet has come along. And with it, many think that these styles of sales are dead. The reason? According to the Corporate Executive Board, Executive Director Matt Dixon, author of *The Challenger Sale*, relationships and solution based pitches are far less relevant in our information age. Today, rather than relying on B2B sellers to perform a needs diagnosis and problem assessment for them, B2B buyers are doing much of this research themselves. And while relationships still matter, the currency of what constitutes a valued relationship has changed dramatically.

Let's look at a similar situation. Years ago, all the solution-selling methods advised vendors to not respond to what are called "blind

Requests for Proposals" or blind RFPs. As with blind RFPs years ago, if you didn't influence a prospect when the prospect created the RFP, chances are you were going to lose.

It's what was then called being "column fodder." The new column fodder is when you haven't done your job in content marketing, such as in e-books, infographics, webinars, etc.

And so, it is now. In today's B2B sales cycle, a prospect has done most of the research already-completing 57 percent of the sales cycle-and has formed opinions about offerings and criteria for selection before a salesperson calls.

In what's recommended in methods called Insight Selling or Challenger Sale, the sales rep uses the occasion to turn a customer with clearly defined requirements into one with emerging needs. Even when sales reps are invited in late, they try to rewind the purchasing decision to a much earlier stage. This type of selling rests on the belief that salespeople must lead with disruptive ideas that will make customers aware of unknown needs.

Summary

"Showing up and throwing up" is still practiced by many sales reps–the bad ones.

They haven't learned the basic lesson of solution selling with needs analysis, discovery, and basic question asking to reveal pain. Successful sales individuals and their organizations have practiced these selling techniques and methodologies for years.

More important, because prospects now complete their own research, these skills become even more critical. The sales rep must not only be a gifted listener, but must also ask questions that can lead to disruption in the prospect's purchasing direction formed by available content on the Internet by the vendors' marketing activities.

THE "CHARLIE CHARLIE" CHALLENGE AND B2B MARKETING LEAD GENERATION

The "Charlie Charlie" Challenge, also known as the Pencil Game or Charlie Pencil, has been around for some time. It's been claimed that the game is an old Mexican tradition, but there's no trace of that on the Internet.

To play the game, take a sheet of paper and draw two lines on it to make a cross. Put a "yes" in the top right and bottom left hand corner, and a "no" in the top left corner and bottom right corner. Place a pencil on the line going across. Then balance another pencil on top of that, along the line going down.

According to the game, to properly summon the demon, you then have to ask, "Charlie, Charlie, can we play?"

The pencils should then start moving. If they go to "yes," the demon is ready and willing to answer your questions. Put the pencil back, and use the same technique to get other answers. If it's a "no," then you'll have to come back later or try again.

When I saw some of the YouTube videos and Facebook posts on the game, as a B2B marketing guy, I thought about lead generation. I know, I know. Call me weird.

But day after day I've entered into conversations about B2B lead generation, and in particular lead scoring, lead nurturing and other lead process items, that make me think we're playing the "Charlie Charlie" Game with leads I've created and handed to sales.

It's like we're simply asking Charlie Spirit if they're good leads or declare them so, as we convince ourselves of their validity owing to a number of factors.

For many companies, the process, despite the acceptance and use of inbound marketing and marketing automation tools, goes like this: Marketing communications creates a campaign, gets lots of leads, and declares victory.

Sales receives the leads and declares them all "sh*t." Marketing then refers back to the campaign to defend its activities. And like the "Charlie Charlie" Challenge, we ask ourselves if they are good and magically, Glengarry leads—the kind that are ready to buy—then, they could close more business.

Success in B2B sales ultimately comes down to the way you manage your sales funnel, and a key part of that is how you source and manage your leads. Which brings us to the importance of getting agreement with sales on what a prospect is, about the buyer's journey, and how leads should get passed to sales.

Marketing communications is in service to sales on this issue. And inevitably, how we score a lead so we don't use the "Charlie Charlie" Challenge to guess, or self-declare, if it's a good lead.

Lead scoring should tell you which leads are ready to buy, which ones need to be nurtured, and sometimes, which ones to ignore. And we all need a system to define hot, warm, and cold leads or A, B, and C, etc. leads.

By categorizing, or scoring leads, you can make the call as to how they should be targeted, and whether leads need to be approached by the sales team, the marketing team, or senior executives.

Lead scoring is successful when leads with higher scores convert into closed, or won, business more often than low-scoring leads. Further, success improves alignment between functions based on adherence to a service-level agreement (SLA).

Analyzing sales velocity and conversion-to-revenue rates is critical to measuring scoring effectiveness and ongoing success. If lead scoring is effective, the process should also include a methodology for optimizing for continued improvement.

But don't take the effort lightly. Lead scoring is one of the more challenging initiatives for most to undertake, as it requires alignment of sales and marketing and a process for change to be truly effective.

Increased sales efficiency through scoring is very achievable. It just requires a commitment to implement properly. Quick and dirty implementations typically won't produce measurable results.

DemandGen International recommends zeroing in on two types of overall "fit" criteria first, and then going deeper with unique profiling questions. The principal criteria are:

1. **Explicit fit criteria** are provided by a prospect. Examples might include company size, industry, the prospect's role, and specific product or service interests. Explicit attributes are typically obtained through website forms when a lead first enters the system.

2. **Implicit behavior criteria** are based on online activity and are often called digital-body language. Examples might include the depth of a website visit, how many times and how recently a prospect visited a website, clicking through nurture emails, registering for webinars, completing certain high-value forms, and even viewing particular areas of the website where a buyer can indicate interest.

No matter how you choose to nurture and score your leads, it's better to nurture and score them than not to do so.

So, stop playing the "Charlie Charlie" Game with lead gen and put in place something that works.

What's a Lead?

S omewhere around 2004, after spending close to 20 years in marketing and various executive sales-leadership positions, I remember
holding a standard weekly sales call and being asked by a salesperson, "What's a lead?" I took the question at face value and was somewhat
shocked that a sales rep of almost equal experience and longevity would
ask such a question.

Well, it turned out, that she was right and I was wrong for being
shocked by the question, especially as we've moved into an age of marketing automation and a more quantitative set of measures for marketing communications.

The question—what's a lead? –is actually a great-and fair-question
that we should be asking ourselves and defining clearly so that we can
move top of the funnel activities effectively through to sales, so that sales
people can make progress on deals through the middle and bottom of
the funnel.

Leads have a long history in B2B marketing. According to recent
surveys, the biggest challenge B2B marketers face with respect to lead
generation is generating high-quality leads.

Traditionally, when I look at the three, primary categories of marketing-communications spending we can all engage in, I put them in three
big buckets: awareness (such as PR, speaking events, blogging, on-line
ads, some aspects of social media, etc.); sales support (data sheets, bro-
chures, case studies, ROI calculators, etc.); and finally, lead generation.

Lead-generation activities are broad and encompass telemarketing, direct mail, email, events like trade shows, inbound calls, search (both SEO and PPC), webinars and seminars.

As B2B marketing has changed, the last category of webinars and seminars has become more important. In some organizations, these activities were left up to the sales organizations and sometimes were referred to as field marketing, since they were considered beneath the corporate marketing part of the organization where members were considered more creative and strategic. Those days are gone. Driving sales and reducing barriers to transactions is key.

An issue with defining what a lead is has to do with the traditional roles, and yes, the friction between sales and marketing. Marketing often exclaims, "We generated tons of leads!" as if to declare success by the volume generated.

At the other end, the receivers of these leads, sales people, often proclaim the opposite. "All these leads are crap" sales people have been heard to say. It's a zero-sum game that produces a losing process with little or no accountability, a lot of frustration, and sadly, no results.

As a result, many frustrated CEO's or executives make one role–the Vice President of Sales and Marketing–or something like this to reduce friction and create singular ownership and accountability.

That is the extent some will go to resolve this issue. But that's a mistake and it's not enough. I believe there are better ways to create cooperation and effectiveness.

What to do then? In our new, digitized world, marketing's job is to keep the sales funnel full of high value leads; the sales team's job is to close new business.

To be clear, let's examine the context about the changing buyers' landscape and create some definitions.

Today, prospects are much more informed about you and your competitor's products and services, have identified their own needs, and started to design their own solutions all before even thinking about talking to a salesperson.

According to a study by the Corporate Executive Board, buyers are now 57 percent of the way toward a buying decision, when they first make contact with a salesperson. Salespeople have no control in this situation, unless they figure out how to add value to the prospect's deci-sion-making process.

Identifying key buying criteria such as the classic IBM created model of budget, authority, need and time frame (BANT) isn't good enough anymore. As a result, leads are no longer just leads. Until recently, if we did any measurement of metrics around leads, we used BANT. With BANT, we could create a system where we could associate some criteria of "hot, warm, or cold" to leads.

BANT still has a use, but it needs to be brought into play differently in light of today's buyer's journey, where prospects are learning much more online before they reach out in a buying process.

One major reason is that by the time a lead is fully "BANT quali-fied," it's probably too late. Your odds of concluding a sale on your terms are greatly diminished, because a competitor has probably established a favored position.

What companies are doing today is essentially breaking down BANT along the buyer's journey so they can capture a prospect's interest and stay involved as a prospect proceeds through the process.

A typical way we see this in today's marketing automation world is as follows:

- **Marketing Qualified Leads (MQL)**: This is a lead that has achieved a certain score based on a predetermined set of criteria and is ready to be handed off to sales. This is essentially discover-ing if there is a need and what level of authority a prospect has. A marketing qualified lead (MQL) might be regarded as someone in the right sort of role at the right sort of company. Plus, this person shows some behavior–clicking in an email and download-ing a whitepaper, reading about one of your solutions–that indi-cates a readiness to be engaged by sales.
- **Sales Accepted Leads (SAL):** Leads accepted by sales for follow-up actions. This is essential for alignment between sales and marketing.
- **Sales Qualified Leads (SQL):** Leads that convert into opportu-nities–either wins or losses. This is where sales also seeks to learn "Budget" and "Time Frame," right sort of role at the right sort

of company, plus this person shows some behavior–clicking in an email and downloading a whitepaper, reading about one of your solutions–that indicates the SQL is ready for sales.

A Sales Accepted Lead "SAL" is one where sales contacts an MQL and decides, "Yes, this is a lead; sales should work." The lead may then go through budget and readiness qualifying to determine if this is a sales qualified lead "SQL" that should be worked to a closed/won revenue opportunity. In this case, it's important to define what is not a marketing qualified lead. Some companies look only for role fit, company fit, and some interest indicators and nothing else. Determining available budget or whether a decision to purchase has been made are sales-lead questions.

It also important to score the leads in each step. Measuring lead effectiveness by assigning a numeric score based on a predefined set of rules effectively removes the subjectivity from qualitative rankings like Hot, Warm and Cold leads. Quantitative lead definitions also reduce the friction between sales and marketing. You may have to guess at first what the criteria are or what the right "number" is to associate with a lead, but just get started and the process will improve over time as you complete more and more sales cycles. It is important to go back and review the leads associated with the wins and losses to refine your criteria.

Now some simple math and an example: Let's assume that your revenue target calls for incremental new revenue of $10 million and that your average deal size is $25,000. This would translate into 400 new deals required to meet this revenue target. Let's further assume that your sales reps can close one out of every four (1:4) well qualified leads. Therefore, to close 400 deals, you'll need to meet your revenue objective of $10 million for the year, you'll need 1,600 Sales Qualified leads (SQL).

So, what's a lead? It could be a MQL, SAL or SQL. Well, it's a lot more complicated an answer than it was before. If done correctly, it will also be more useful to your business, to your salespeople, and to the revenue of your company. Spend some time on the definitions and the results will be well worth the effort

Bad News Early is Good News: Avoiding Sudden Turns

W e've all been there at one time or another. You're at the end of a sales cycle, working on the last parts of a contract. You can sense the celebration for what has been a very long process. And then it happens. Your prospect suddenly changes his or her mind.

"But how?" you ask. "Why?"

You were down to the last three items in the contract negotiations. After weeks of back and forth and the compilation of months of diligent work, the end was almost at hand.

And just like that, the prospect wants out of the deal.

I remember the last time this happened to me. After a few days of corresponding back and forth on the contract items, I received an email that read: "We will not proceed." Ouch!

I was stunned, not only because the deal was not moving forward, but how the decision was communicated to me. After all that time and money, I was told it was over in an email. Not even a call.

Selling is a tough business. I don't have to tell you that. There are no "easy sales" out there. I believe all B2B marketing and selling is based on relationships. Even in this high-tech world of digital marketing, where social media reigns, our interactions are based on creating relationships. And what's the basis of these relationships?

The basis is trust. I call the process of building successful relationships a "trust bank account." And make no mistake about it. Both sides must make more deposits than withdrawals. When you're in sales, you deal with all kinds of personalities. Your job is to make sure that despite all of those back and forth discussions, the "trust bank account" is built up.

In the story I just referenced, there was a "trust bank account." But owing to some last-minute miscommunications, my client made a 100-percent withdrawal, a sudden turn. Maybe it was cold feet. Who knows? But when something like this happens, both sides lose. The transaction isn't completed and yet my customers' needs remain. Sure, everyone can stitch some set of actions together to move forward in another manner, but ephemeral decisions to stop a process can do long-term harm.

That's the way "carbon-based units" process information. We react when we're under pressure or aren't ready to act or make a decision. Not everyone's communications skills (see that email notification above) are capable of thinking through the impact or results of their actions.

I probably shouldn't have been surprised. A good sales rep should always confirm where he stands in the complex sales process – during each step and after every meeting. Losing a deal at the last minute is unforgivable, no matter the reasons. Clearly, I didn't reconfirm the benefits of moving forward to minimize the objections that would have prevented a 100-percent withdrawal from the "trust bank account."

That's on me.

What could I have done? I should have reconfirmed the deal in writing and in person. Instead, I relied on the investment that was made to date by the other party as evidence of commitment. Confirming letters are key at every step of the sales cycle. While not having one in this case, especially as the deal was closing, wasn't necessary; it should have been warranted given this was the first time my prospect was making a purchase. He clearly wasn't ready. Honestly, he may never be.

So, what is a confirming letter? It is actually a simple, yet often forgotten tool in the selling process. At the end of every meeting, tell your prospect you'll write him a letter or email that reviews what was said in the discussion. This will confirm your understanding of where things are in the discussion.

Within 24 hours of the meeting, write this note and place it in your customer/prospect file folder or your sales automation system. Believe me, it's important. I've found these to be incredibly important, not just at the end of a process, but during each and every stage.

I've found prospects correct me as to my perceptions or even correct what they told me. Either way, it's important. Remember: Bad news early is good news.

Make sure you and your prospect are in alignment. That's important at each and every step of the sales cycle. It's a simple tool that will make sure you're building your "trust bank account" and avoiding surprises as your deal progresses. A small amount of your time will pay huge dividends.

Don't be surprised as I was. Build your "trust bank account" with each of your prospects or existing customers by taking a few minutes to write a confirming letter or email after each meeting or phone call.

It's a lesson learned, one that will help you avoid those sudden, sharp turns in the road.

Need Some FAB?

I n most peoples' minds, when you say the term, FAB, you're talking about a laundry detergent by Colgate Palmolive. Or you might be referring to a recent e-commerce company that spent $200 million in two years only to declare, "We have no business model" and then shutting down the company that later became resurrected. When I hear the term, FAB, however, I hear it as an acronym for Features, Advantages and Benefits.

When I was a young, retail salesperson, I worked at a local Pittsburgh based music store. I remember one Saturday morning when a sales representative from St. Louis Music came in to our little music shop to teach us how to sell the new line of Alvarez brand guitars we were going to begin carrying.

We carried and sold some of the best guitar brands, including Gibson, Martin, Guild and others. At the time, in the mid 70's, Alvarez wanted to compete with these guitar market giants. The Alvarez brand was ultimately played over the years by Bono (The Edge), Johnny Cash, Crosby, Stills & Nash, Ani DiFranco, Jerry Garcia, Paul McCartney, Monte Montgomery, Carlos Santana, and Bob Weir.

To make that kind of head way in the guitar business, Alvarez sent its distributor sales representatives to teach us the basics of sales. And that began with FAB.

We huddled in one of the small lesson rooms to hear this presentation on how to pitch the guitars. And the importance of FAB was revealed to us. The representative asked us to FAB everything we saw. "FAB this music stand." "FAB this carpet." FAB this ash tray." He emphasized the importance of being able to think and talk like this about any object, so that we were really prepared when prospects came into the store to discuss guitars.

Of course, we learned all the features, advantages and benefits of the Alvarez guitar line and we could talk about them in detail and relay that information to prospects.

The FAB for the Alvarez guitars was not only better and different from the major brands, there were also more Alvarez guitars than competing models.

The lesson wasn't lost on me. I've spent a career in sales and marketing, and FAB is still essential for me to unlock the value proposition for many of the products and companies I've represented.

A key lesson: No one buys features. This is particularly true in B2B marketing and sales. People, and companies, buy benefits.

The underlying lesson was this: Practicing FAB was, and is, highly important.

Most of us confuse or don't really understand the difference between features, advantages, and benefits.

The key to advantages is being able to state what differences these features make to the customer. *"And the key for benefits is..."* How will the outcomes be better because of these differences?

Let's look at these three words:

- **Features** are one of the easier things to identify. Features are facts or characteristics about your business, products, and services. Here's an example of a feature that should be familiar: "His mobile phone has e-mail support." Features tend to be factual, and aren't connected to a prospect's need.
- **Advantages** are what features do. An advantage describes how a product, or a product feature, can be used or can help a buyer. Advantages are more persuasive than features and most advantages can be expressed in this form: Because of (feature), you can (advantage). For example, "Because this mobile phone has continuous access to your e-mails, you can keep in touch with your business on the move."

- **Benefits** answer why someone should value an advantage. A benefit connects the facts about your product to a solution for your client. For example, "Continuous access to your e-mails means you can be confident to respond promptly if a customer sends you an e-mail."

Here's the full FAB statement:

"Our mobile phones offer continuous access to your emails. Now you will be able to have access to your emails wherever you go. And continuous access to your e-mails means you can be confident that if a customer sends you an e-mail, you can respond quickly."

Can you see how this helps to connect a prospect's desire to your product? Of course, if that's something your prospects or target market don't value, then it doesn't matter.

Blending FAB Statements into Marketing Messages

Once you identify your various features, advantages, and benefits, you can start compiling them into succinct marketing and sales messages. The FAB Statements exercise will help you connect better with your prospective clients.

Try it yourself. Put together a list of your product features. Then go back and add the corresponding advantages of each and, finally, the benefits. More important, put yourself into your prospect's shoes as you develop these.

Remember:

Because your product has a FEATURE,
You will be able to enjoy an ADVANTAGE.
What this means to you is a BENEFIT.

Have a FABulous time selling.

THE ART OF THE PITCH

"**O**bserve the world around you—everything you do, and especially everything you hate to do." ~ Aaron Patzer, Founder, MINT, Preambler

You need to address three items here:

Type in "The art of the pitch" in Google, and you'll find more than 94 million entries and links. What I have to add to this subject has probably been stated many, many times by those more capable or better versed than I.

First, entire books and courses have been devoted to this subject; so, one, simple chapter won't do the subject justice. Think of this as "Cliff Notes" for pitching, an entry to a subject that requires a lot of commitment.

Second, as you read these sources you'll see not only a convergence of ideas, suggestions and recommendations such as fewer words, more pictures, you'll also see some strong differences. You'll have to choose what's good for you and what works for you. As I like to say about advertising, "like" has nothing to do with it; advertising is about what's effective.

Third, you should consider another element: Time. Not only how much time you have to pitch, which is very important, but also this: What we consider a great pitch today may not have been a great pitch 10 years ago or 10 years in the future. Making a pitch isn't something you learn once.

And finally, consider that best of all statements about marketing and pitches in general: You can't shine a turd. You can do a great pitch, but if you don't have, or can't deliver, the goods, a great pitch won't make up for it. I can also guarantee you that a bad pitch, or even a mediocre one, can harm a great offering.

Background on Pitching

Now, I'm going to share with you some prescriptive information about giving a great pitch.

Let's start with a common issue for pitches: fear. It takes a lot of guts, or foolishness, to give a pitch. Many of us are fearful of giving pitches. According to most studies, people's number one fear is public speaking. Number two is death. Does that seem right?

This means that for the average person, if you attend the wake of a dead person, you're better off being the one in the casket than the one giving the eulogy. (Thank you Jerry Seinfield.)

Fear can be good as well. Use it to your advantage. I've found the best way to overcome the fear of public speaking is to practice. And then practice. And then practice some more. Stand in front of a mirror and do the pitch. Video record yourself and watch it. You can learn a lot about improving your pitch before someone else does it for you.

And take the prep advice someone provides seriously. Even if you're a pro speaker and do it a lot, and people say you're good at it, preparation is still the key. Think about it: Football players spend a week practicing before a three-hour game on Sunday. Symphonies spend a week rehearsing for a concert they'll give over a weekend.

These are just two examples of top professionals who practice, regardless of their talent and experience. You should, too. When you're ready, the pitch should be second nature. It should be a part of you. You should be able to do it anytime, anywhere, on demand. You should know how the audience is going to react to any portion of the pitch. Not practicing is the Number-1 reason people deliver presentations poorly. So, take your vitamins, exercise, and practice your pitch. It's all good.

Now, let's look at another important part of a pitch. And let's say you're in the investing business. The single, most important thing that potential investors, or the equivalent, want to know about is you.

Think about it in these terms: They're going to invest their money and trust you to take it and make more for them, much more, in a shorter period of time than they can gain from other forms of investment.

Do yourself a favor: Take your credit cards, and whatever cash you have in your purse or wallet, and stroke yourself a check for $1,000.00, or a significant amount, and set all of that down in front of you. Now do your pitch with the money sitting in front of you, and ask yourself if you're worth it. Would you give yourself that money?

Better yet, ask your wife, husband, significant other, or a close friend to do the same. And see if any one of them would part with that money. If you, or a close friend, won't invest in your pitch, don't think about asking others.

So, to have a successful pitch in whatever time you have, you need to get across a number of different characteristics about yourself. You can't just say, "I'm a good person, and you should invest in me." What do you think these characteristics are? Consider these:

- Integrity,
- Passion,
- Experience,
- Knowledge,
- Skills,
- Leadership,
- Commitment,
- Vision,
- Realism, and
- Coachability…to listen.

So, in whatever way we get across about a business and an opportunity, we need to convey these qualities directly or indirectly in our pitches as well. We want to ensure that what we present underscores these characteristics and that we demonstrate these as we pitch.

Now, on to the mechanics of a presentation. There are lots of outlines of great pitches. Here are a few I like:

- Guy Kawasaki: https://guykawasaki.com/the-only-10-slides-you-need-in-your-pitch/
- One Match Ventures: http://onematchventures.com/the-best-startup-investor-pitch-deck-how-to-present-to-angels-vcs/.
- Examples: http://bestpitchdecks.com Again, neither comprehensive nor exhaustive, but some good ones.

The 9 Elements of a Pitch

1. Introduction,
2. Problem statement,
3. Solution,
4. How does it work
5. How do you make money
6. Your market,
7. Marketing,
8. Business economics, and
9. Conclusion.

If you had to, you could reduce this list to Problem/Solution/Money. Let's dig a little deeper:

Introduction

Anyone interested in you, your invention or your company is looking at the 4M's. As Venture Capitalist Mark Suster states: Management Team, Momentum, Market and Money.

So, I want to understand the answer to the question, "Why you?" right off the bat, and that's why I want to know about you and the team first. It may also be good to tell me about your passion or your experience, and of course, the problem solving and complementary skills and experience of the team.

Problem statement

I love starting with the problem. Better yet, I love telling a story about the problem–something your audience can relate to. A story is much more compelling than a collection of facts. And it's been shown to be more effective and memorable.

Let's say you're the CEO of Foobar, Inc., and your company makes HR Performance Review software. Maybe you tell a story of about two employees engaged in a performance review. And your story is, "Meet Joe and Mary. Joe is doing her annual performance review. Joe hates doing performance reviews. And so does Mary."

Everyone hates performance reviews, because they take up so much time, and because it's hard to remember what each of your dozen coworkers accomplished last year. Research indicates that employees spend 3 percent of their year on performance reviews, which results in $15 billion of wasted productivity every year. That's good storytelling.

Solution

Next is your solution. Make it clear. What's your value proposition? Make it clear. Some folks think it should be so clear that your mother should be able to understand it. That can be a good litmus test.

If we go back to my example of Foobar, Inc., it could sound something like this: "We are building software that streamlines the performance review process. Our tool is extremely easy to use and cuts review times by 80 percent. It also allows employees to submit feedback whenever they want, instead of during a magical once a year period.

How does it work

It's important here not to get in the weeds. Don't make it complicated. Keep it simple. And if you have an offering that lends itself to a demo, make sure it's canned. No live demos.

How do you make money

The most significant goal of a startup is finding a scalable and repeatable business model. We want to understand how you make money. How does your business work? What are the "goes-in-zas" and the "goes-out-zas"? Understand how the business scales and makes money.

Your market

This part of the pitch is all about three things:

- Who is/are your customers?
- How big is your market? and
- Who is/are your competitor(s)?

Anyone interested in you, your invention, or your company is looking at the 4M's.

Again, a As Venture Capitalist Mark Suster, states: "Management Team, Momentum, Market and Money."

- How are you going to reach your customers?
- How are you going to reach your early adopters?
- What is your customer-acquisition plan?

Be specific about how you contact (lead gen) prospects, and the time it'll take to acquire them, as well as the cost of acquisition. And remember, most investors dislike ideas that have a high burn rate for marketing. Important: If you have early adopters–paid or not–tell that story and how they'll help get others.

Business economics

Then, there's the ask: How much money will you need and how much are you giving up (equity)? What are you going to do with that cash? How far will that take you? Give us your forecast and projections, and please, we don't need eye charts and Excel tables.

Walk us through the economics. Investors are looking for key numbers:

1. What is the initial required investment to start your business?
2. What's your pricing strategy?
3. When do you forecast to break even?, and
4. When will you be cash-flow positive?

Conclusion

Show a graph of where and when your customer-acquisition costs are going to decline. Conclusion: If you don't ask, you don't get. So, get ready. As you finish, give a reason for us to believe that you are ready to... ROCK!

End your presentation by mentioning how you, with investors' help, can be successful as no other. Again, be specific. What can their money and they, along with you, accomplish?

And of course, say, "Thank you."

Pet Peeves that Kill Pitches

A lot can go wrong in a pitch. So, practice. Did I mention that? But also try to avoid these mistakes:

Jargon and acronyms. Not everyone knows what you do or comes from your space. Spell out the TLA's–Three Letter Acronyms–at least the first time.

Too many words per slide, with no graphics. Ever see Steve Jobs's pitch? It was usually a colorful screen or a pic of the product in the background. You're focused on– guess what?– him, and what he had to say. Fewer words are better. Use short bullet-point material, if you have to.

Unrealistic projections. Don't make them. The best projections have rationales top down and bottom up. To say, "If we just capture 1 percent of the market," is not a winner. No one walks away winning a market at 1 percent of anything. If you're really as good as you say you are, and the market is that important, you will win big and so will your investors. And that's not with 1 percent market share.

No reading your notes and no reading slides. Know your pitch. Don't read your pitch. Note cards are so 1960's. Look into the judges' eyes, connect with them, show the passion you have and your control and knowledge of your subject.

No mistakes or misspellings. It's easy to spell check. I know I don't spell check many times. I hope I did here. But it's similar to the old Tom Peters story. When he would see a dirty tray on an airliner, he would wonder how they took care of the engine. Check your pitch deck. Better yet, have someone else check it.

And there are more things I hated about your pitch. Check them out here: http://articles.bplans.com/10-things-i-hated-about-your-business-pitch/.

Whew! That's a lot. As I said, it's a big subject. I hope this was a good refresher for you or a good starting point for those who have yet to pitch. Either way, good selling and good pitching!

WANT TO MAKE IT MEMORABLE? TELL A STORY

Let's begin with a story. In 1983, in an alley outside a grubby pub in Boston, Frank Johnson drew his fishing knife and faced the barroom bully, Alan Caldwell. The much taller and more muscled Caldwell lunged at Johnson, and Johnson's four-inch blade punctured the skin and muscle of Caldwell's abdomen and ended his life.

At the ensuing murder trial, witnesses were interviewed and the blurry events of that night slowly came into focus: Johnson was speaking to a woman in the bar and Caldwell became verbally upset with him. Johnson left the bar but returned later that night with the knife. Caldwell challenged Johnson to step outside. Some witnesses saw Caldwell draw a razor, but others denied this.

The crucial question: Was it murder or self-defense?

The jury heard the evidence and finally arrived at a decision: 63 percent of the jurors agreed it was murder.

But this was no ordinary trial. It was a mock trial staged by researchers with a jury made up of university students learning the persuasive power of storytelling. The trial was repeated, but this time, the prosecuting attorneys presented their arguments in a story format. And when the jury returned, 78 percent of the jurors agreed it was murder. The storytelling format made the prosecutor's argument more persuasive.

The mock trial was repeated a third time. This time, the defense used a storytelling approach.

Now, when the jury returned, only 31 percent of the jurors were convinced it was murder.

The results were sobering: Whichever lawyer used a storytelling approach, the jury was swayed toward agreeing with the evidence presented.

Stories are powerful. They can convict a man to prison or set him free. And what about you? Do you have ideas with which you want your audience to understand and agree? Can a story be the difference between a successful recommendation and a failed one?

As business professionals–especially if we have technical backgrounds–we often tell ourselves that we shouldn't tell stories in a business setting. Here are what I call "story-telling myths":

- Stop wasting my time. A story takes too long.
- Stories are false and make-believe.
- Just give us the facts.

None of these storytelling myths are accurate. Quite the contrary, storytelling is an effective tool used to convey messages.

Stories are:

- Easy to understand,
- Persuasive, and
- Memorable.

Here's another story to explain why this is true:

In a faraway land, a boy went to learn at the feet of a wise man day after day. The wise man instructed the boy through stories. One day, the boy asked the wise man, "Master, why do you always teach through stories? Would it not be faster to teach me directly?" To this, the wise man answered, "Please bring me some tea." The boy rose and prepared a cup of tea in a white, china cup. The wise man took the cup from the boy, sipped some tea, and then asked, "Why did you bring me a cup when I only asked for tea?"

A story is like a cup. It's the brain's natural container for holding knowledge.

In a moving scene in the movie, *Saving Mr. Banks*, Walt Disney, played by Tom Hanks, says to P.L. Travers, author of Mary Poppins, played by Emma Thompson, "That's what storytellers do. We restore order to imagination. We instill hope again and again."

And that's what a presentation needs to do: Tell a story that reignites an audience's imagination and enables the audience to see your solution as part of their story.

Elements of a Good Story

There are many ways to construct a good story. Here's one:

Set-up

- Introduce the characters and setting, communicate to your audience the situation in which the story begins, and presents some sort of problem or tension.

Build-up

- You then build up the tension you've created, perhaps with events that challenge the characters in unexpected ways.
- A plot can involve a problem, issue, concern, challenge, dilemma, or paradox with specific obstacles to overcome.

Payoff

- And finally, often after a few rounds of build up, you must provide your audience with some sort of payoff.

The good news. Here's a story construction you already know. The story of Cinderella:

Set-up

- Once upon a time there lived an unhappy young girl. Her mother was dead, and her father had married a widow with two daughters. Her stepmother didn't like her one little bit. But she showered her daughters with everything–dresses, shoes, delicious food, soft beds, and every home comfort.

Build-up

- There is going to be a ball, which the stepmother and her daughters don't want to let Cinderella attend.
- Cinderella finds a way to attend the ball in disguise.
- She meets the prince, and they fall in love.
- She flees at midnight and returns to her slavery, without the prince ever learning her identity.
- The prince searches and searches, but cannot find her.

Payoff

- The prince finally does find her and makes her a princess.

Your Cinderella Story

Think about this: After a presentation, 63 percent of listeners remember a story. Only 5 percent remember statistics. So, the next time you're asked to do a presentation, think about a story you can tell.

There are 6 typical business stories that you can plug the setup-build up-payoff process into:

- "Who-I-Am" stories explain who you are as a person.
- "Why-I-Am-Here" stories communicate why you're here, and their aim is to replace suspicion with trust. People want to know, "What's in it for me?" but they also want to know, "What's in it for you?"

- "Teaching Stories" create an experience that transforms listeners or readers.
- "Vision Stories" inspire people and encourage them to feel hope or happiness.
- "Values-in-Action Stories" reinforce the values you want to demonstrate to your audience or have them think about.
- "I-Know-What-You-Are-Thinking" stories allow you to address others' objections, suspicions, questions, or concerns before they voice them.

If you want to learn more about the power of storytelling, check out this link: http://www.ted.com/talks/andrew_stanton_the_clues_to_a_great_story.html.

Good luck on telling your stories.

Are You a Member of the Sales-Prevention Team?

I really enjoy Dunkin' Donuts tea. I know that's crazy, because they have great coffee, donuts, of course, and other treats. But it's their tea that I really enjoy.

The company has done a great job of remaking itself after a near-death experience before 2006, when management made the decision to move from donuts to coffee.

In moving to coffee, they found a new competitor. You may have heard of them: Starbucks. And there's one thing Starbucks does better than Dunkin Donuts: service. Please understand this is a general statement. I'm sure you can recall a bad incident or even several at a Starbucks. But in general, service at Starbucks, especially relative to Dunkin Donuts, is just better.

I regularly see seven people working behind the counter at Dunkin Donuts and one at the cash register. And a line out the door. I've experienced this is at multiple locations I visit. It's systematic or cultural or something. But this isn't good business.

When there's a customer at the door, the people who are exchanging their money for your products or services, you should be able to take that money and provide service in a timely manner. Nothing's more frustrating than standing in line watching someone with a clipboard filling out forms and someone cleaning a machine, or whatever.

Whatever they are doing is not about exchanging money for goods and services. And yes, I get that these other activities need to be done, and in a cost-effective manner, but for goodness sake, let's not have more people behind the counter than in front of the counter, and still a line out the door. The back-office administrative chores, while significant, essential and important, don't exist without the front office chores.

This is not a unique problem. Many business-to-business (B2B) organizations, in addition to business-to-consumer (B2C) businesses, suffer from the inability to focus on customers, and to service their needs, quickly and efficiently.

I have been in many a company where there truly have been "sales prevention teams." These teams come in many forms, but their behaviors are consistent. Like the rule readers who follow policy over good judgment. Is there anything worse than hearing, "We shouldn't have sold that deal, not because it was oversold, but because we can't get out of our way to take the customers' money.

Admittedly, many salespeople will sell anything whether it exists or not, and yes, there is good revenue and bad revenue. Please see my post, "Good Revenue vs. Bad Revenue."

So yes, we do need to stay focused on selling "what's on the truck." Agreed.

But at the same time, we can't allow a back office/administrative bureaucracy and rules that overrun the ability to get results and satisfy customers.

We must be ready to take the deal, when it does fit our criteria and is something we sell, as well. It's so hard to find the right customers and get them to the point where they are ready to part with money. It amazes me to no end when a business has spent money building the right product, marketing to find the right prospect, and selling to gain the right customer, and service people can't get out of their own way to ensure the customer can be served.

As I've stated in other chapters, my definition of marketing is about removing barriers to transactions. I jokingly refer to this as "Coticchia's Claim." My definition is shorter and broader than most. But unlike the others, my definition attempts to be more inclusive of marketing than simply the communications or advertising aspects of marketing.

In reducing barriers, a company and its management must think through the 4 P's—product, price, promotion, and place–and look for ways to efficiently and effectively serve customers. That includes administrative, legal, governance and compliance that *serve the business* but *are not the business.*

That's a distinction–serving the business vs. being the business–that needs to be clearer in many organizations. Or in essence, we've created a sales-prevention team.

WE WENT THROUGH 13 SALESPEOPLE, AND NONE OF THEM WAS SUCCESSFUL. SO, THE PRODUCT OR THE MARKET MUST BE AT FAULT.

N ot so fast.

I love it when I hear early stage-entrepreneurs' statements like the headline above, as if it's scientific evidence that we haven't hired the right salesperson or are not using the right sales process.

Sure, intellectually we can say, "What are the chances of hiring 13 bad reps in 2 years?" Even a blind squirrel finds a nut every once in a while, right? Let's think about that.

Hiring good salespeople is one of the most difficult things a company has to do. Period. Typically, companies need to go through three salespeople to find one successful one with long-term closing power.

This hard fact can take its toll on early-stage companies with limited budgets that can only afford small teams and can't afford to make any mistakes that result in revenue getting delayed down the road.

First, let's discuss how many types of reps you could potentially hire? Well, it turns out there are ten categories of sales. This equates to more than 1,024 specific types of salespersons or two to the 10th degree.

All you need to do is try to hire those who check off the most skills needed for your specific business. This is just one of many reasons why it's hard to hire a good rep.

And if that isn't difficult enough, let's add to it that you're hiring for a startup. Let's define what a startup is, and we will use what Eric Ries, Silicon Valley entrepreneur and author, states: *"A startup is a human institution designed to deliver a new product or service under conditions of extreme uncertainty. "*

And let's add to that Steve Blank, startup guru, who adds about why startups exist: *"A startup is an organization formed to search for a repeatable and scalable business model."*

Let's add these together: Your business is in search of a repeatable and scalable business model, under conditions of extreme uncertainty, and you can choose from 1,024 different types to help you achieve that model defined from a sales perspective.

If you get the right model, so to speak, you still need to figure out how it can be successful, because you don't know and you're in search of it. According to experts in the hiring field, the reality is this: As well as you screen candidates and ask all the right questions, you're only going to get it right one in every three (good) or four (typical) attempts, based on average historical experience.

If I remember my probability and statistics right, each hire you make is not a conditional effect, and therefore not dependent on the previous decision. The probability of hiring one bad person out of 13 is 1/13. Hiring decisions are independent decisions. Like flipping a coin. Again, the probability of hiring the right person is one out of four. If there is someone better at stats feel free to correct me.

Thinking that the number of reps you have, and the relative level of success they obtain, is a reflection of your product or market is like saying that the more money you raise will predict your success as a business. The fact is that the amount of money startups raise in their seed and Series A rounds is inversely correlated with success.

Need I remind anyone that, yes, you can have great sales with a sh*t product. Just think of popcorn in theaters, bottled water (a questionable value), and International Star Registry (This organization has been naming stars since 1979). Think about that. And of course, cigarettes.

Hiring sales reps for your startup is tough stuff. You can burn through lots of reps and waste time and money that's precious for a startup. Don't jump to the conclusion that if your salespeople can't sell what's on the truck, that it's what you are selling that stinks.

TAKE THE RISK. TAKE THE CHANCE. DOING SO COULD CHANGE YOUR LIFE

I n 1997, Steve Van Zandt delivered a speech for inducting The Rascals into the Rock and Roll Hall of Fame. For those of you who may not recognize the name, Steven Van Zandt is an American musician, songwriter, arranger, record producer, actor, and radio disc jockey, who frequently goes by the stage names, Little Steven or Miami Steve. He is a member of Bruce Springsteen's E Street Band, in which he plays guitar and mandolin.

A longtime fan of what were originally called "The Young Rascals," Van Zandt campaigned for the group to be inducted into the Rock and Roll Hall of Fame. In 1997, they were voted in, and Van Zandt gave an infamous speech that you can watch here:

https://www.bing.com/videos/search?q=Van+Zandt+speech+1997+Rock+and+Roll+Hall+of+Fame&&view=detail&mid=CF88D4300250D1 A7A1C8CF88D4300250D1A7A1C8&&FORM=VDRVRV

I'm a huge Springsteen fan, and I love a lot of the artists related to Bruce, including Southside Johnny, Joe Grushecky, and Van Zandt himself, to name just a few.

Van Zandt has enjoyed many achievements in his life. Did you know his series, "Lilyhammer," was the first series to allow binge watching and all-at-once viewing that we all love on Netflix? But his induction speech for the Rascals may be the one that stands out for me. Why?

Van Zandt took a chance with the speech. He didn't need to do it and he didn't have to do it either. He started by following his passion, music. And part of this was his love for the Rascals and their importance in rock and roll. When they were inducted into the Rock and Roll Hall of Fame, they asked Van Zandt to do the induction speech for them.

What's amazing about that?

His speech landed him his role on *The Sopranos,* regarded by some as one of the greatest television series of all time. The series also won a multitude of awards, including Peabody Awards for its first two seasons, 21 Emmy Awards, and five Golden Globe Awards. The series creator, David Chase, watched the broadcast of the Rascal's induction ceremony on VH1, saw Van Zandt's speech, and decided to offer him a role on *The Sopranos,* even though Van Zandt had no acting experience.

That's what taking a chance can do.

Early in the 90's, I received a call from someone looking for a job. Back then, I was running a small startup, and the person who called me was looking for a sales role. We lacked a salesperson at the time, so I took the call and set up an appointment to meet this person.

Several years later, when I was looking for a new gig, this same gentleman offered me a consulting role. To make a long story short, I ended up on his board of directors, serving for 17 years until the company was recently acquired.

I had nothing to offer that person in terms of what he was seeking, but I took the chance–the risk, if you can call it that–and this turned into nearly two decades of a business and personal relationship that I value highly.

Although overused, Wayne Gretzky's quote still holds true: "You miss 100 percent of the shots you don't take." If Steve Van Zandt had said, "Let some rock icon from the 60's induct the Rascals." Or if he had brushed off the request with "I'm too busy," he would have never had the career trajectory he enjoys today.

Yes, there are plenty of ways to waste our time as well. And yes, we do need to focus on accomplishing our goals. But never fear to take a chance once in a while.

It may rock your world. And who knows where responding to a friendly request will lead you?

Last week, I sat in on a presentation where one of the speakers was discussing how "hip" and trendy doing a startup is these days. She said, tongue in cheek, "Everyone needs to have a house, two cars, kids, a dog and a startup."

We've seen the popularity of startups come and go over the years. And certainly, I have since I did my first startup in 1985. The late 90s were exceptional. And the time we are living in now may be a close second as it continues to be a good market for starting new businesses.

Having seen a lot of folks come and go through startups I've been involved with, I've gathered some perspectives about startups that may be useful, if you're considering starting one or joining one.

Here you go:

1. **A startup is not a lottery ticket.** The unfortunate aspect of startups is that they can attract a lot of get-rich-quick people. If a startup isn't a fit for you, you'll know, and your peers, bosses and employees will know as well. Don't try to kid yourself or others.

2. **Startups aren't glamorous.** If your idea of glamor is sweating how you're going to make payroll, working 10- to 12-hour work days, 6 and 7 days a week, and making less money than you could make at a larger, established organization, then you're in.

3. Sure, there's the occasional award dinner held by your local tech organization, or you may get mentioned on a list of published superstars. But recognitions like these are not what a startup is about. And most of what it takes to do a startup isn't glamorous.

4. **Cash, cash, cash is what matters.** If you're a founder or senior leader and you're creating what Bill Aulet of M.I.T. calls an "innovation-driven enterprise," think about the likes of Google or Uber. You'll constantly be raising money from friends, family, fools, angels, institutional investors, strategic investors and more. Every day, when you're done with that job, you can begin your other job, the one you haven't left yet.

Fact is, cash is a constant concern for startups, from what your burn rate is to thinking about where you are with cash flow, to knowing what you've sold, and when can you collect the cash. Running a startup is a constant job and you're under pressure day in and day out.

So, if you like knowing that every month or two weeks the salary you were to be paid for your work is *there*, deposited in your bank account, a startup is likely.

Stay focused, but *do everything*. To be successful in a startup, no matter your role, you'll need to focus on what matters and do the things that count. Everyone will tell you that. They'll tell you to "focus on the segment of the market that'll drive sales" or "focus on the functionality in your product that'll deliver differentiated value to your customers." And you'll hear, "Focus on what you're good at."

And when you realize you don't have all the resources you need and you can't afford to buy them, you'll know that you need to be the greatest utility player ever!

And if the people who tell you to focus are investors in your startup, they'll tell you things like "get it done" or "do whatever it takes."

A startup can teach you thousands of lessons. Making the leap and creating a company is one of the most exhilarating life and business experiences you'll ever have. But, what isn't said about starting a company or joining a startup is important. Keep that in mind before you make the leap.

And once your startup is underway, pay attention to what you didn't know when you started, but had to learn t from others you could learn from.

Section 2 Quiz

Test Your Knowledge from Section 2

1. When you have a product or service that's a solution for customers, they can choose to do four things. What are they?
2. When defining your product or service, what three questions should you ask and answer? And why?
3. A marketer for a startup company describes his or her company's product as having something for everyone. What's right or wrong with this market description and why?
4. Neil Rackham's SPIN selling model provides four questions to ask on a sales call. What are these four questions?
5. To be effective, B2B sales leads need to be scored. What three things should your scoring system tell you?
6. Sales leads may be Marketing Qualified Leads (MQL), Sales Accepted Leads (SAL), and Sales Qualified Leads. Describe each of these types of sales leads.
7. What should you do immediately after a sales meeting?
8. In B2B sales, what do people and companies actually buy? Features? Advantages? Benefits? How do you describe each of these?
9. What audience pet peeves should you avoid when giving a sales pitch?
10. If your hire 13 salespeople for your startup, the probability is that one will be a bad hire is 1/13. True or false? And why?

Answers to Section 2 Quiz

1. Customers can buy from you, buy from a competitor, buy a substitute–a different way to solve the same problem–or do nothing. In this case, your competitor is apathy. (**So, I have This Idea for a New Product, And I Wanted to Know, "What Do You Think About It?"**)

2. So, think: What problem does your product solve? What need does your product meet? What want does your product fulfill? And get that to a focused list that you can absolutely make sure resonates with your customers. (**The Secret 8 Steps to Startup, Customer Attraction and Sales**)

3. It's wrong, because everything to everyone means nothing to no one. A marketer must choose to be as specific as possible on who buys his or her product, and then focus on these buyers, to the exclusion of all others. (**The Secret 8 Steps to Startup Customer Attraction and Sales**)

4. S stands for Situation Questions. P stands for Problem Questions. I stands for Implication Questions. N stands for Need Payoff Questions. (**B2B Selling: Stop Showing Up and Throwing Up**)

5. Lead scoring should tell you which leads are ready to buy, which ones need to be nurtured, and sometimes, which ones to ignore. And we all need a system to define hot, warm, and cold leads or A, B, and C leads. (**The "Charlie Charlie" Challenge And B2B Marketing Lead Generation**)

6. Marketing Qualified Leads (MQL): These leads have achieved a certain score based on a predetermined set of criteria and are ready to be handed off to sales. Sales Accepted Leads (SAL): These are leads accepted by sales for follow-up actions. Sales Qualified Leads (SQL): These leads convert into opportunities--either wins or losses. (**What's A Lead?**)

7. At the end of every meeting, tell your prospect you'll write him or her a letter or send an email that reviews what was said in the discussion. This will confirm your understanding

of where things are in your discussions. (**Bad News Early is Good News: Avoiding Sudden Turns**)

8. Companies and people buy benefits. Features are one of the easier things to identify. Advantages are what features do. Benefits answer why someone should value an advantage. (**Need Some FAB?**)

9. Jargon and acronyms. Too many words per slide and no graphics. Unrealistic projections, Reading your notes and reading slides. Mistakes or misspellings. (**The Art of the Pitch**)

10. Each hire you make is not a conditional effect, and therefore, not dependent on the previous decision. The probability of hiring one bad person out of 13 is 1/13. (**We Went Through 13 Salespeople and None of Them Were "Successful." So, The Product or The Market Must Be at Fault**)

Made in the USA
Columbia, SC
21 November 2018